THE

FRUSTRATED SONGWRITER'S

HANDBOOK

THE
FRUSTRATED
SONGWRITER'S
HANDBOOK

A RADICAL GUIDE TO CUTTING LOOSE, OVERCOMING BLOCKS, & WRITING THE BEST SONGS OF YOUR LIFE

Backbeat
Books
San Francisco

By Karl Coryat & Nicholas Dobson

Illustrations by Bunny Knutson

Published by Backbeat Books
600 Harrison Street, San Francisco, CA 94107
www.backbeatbooks.com
email: books@musicplayer.com

An imprint of the Music Player Network
Publishers of *Guitar Player*, *Bass Player*, *Keyboard*, and other magazines
United Entertainment Media, Inc.
A CMP Information company

CMP
United Business Media

Distributed to the book trade in the US and Canada by
Publishers Group West, 1700 Fourth Street, Berkeley, CA 94710

Distributed to the music trade in the US and Canada by
Hal Leonard Publishing, P.O. Box 13819, Milwaukee, WI 53213

Text and cover design by Richard Leeds — bigwigdesign.com
Back cover photos by Richard Leeds — bigwigdesign.com
Composition by Brad Greene

ISBN 10: 0-87930-879-6
ISBN 13: 978-0-87930-879-7

Printed in the United States of America
08 09 10   5 4 3 2

This book is dedicated to Michael Mellender,

the meanest, baddest speed-composer in the whole damn Society.

CONTENTS

I N T R O D U C T I O N

WHAT EXACTLY IS A "FRUSTRATED SONGWRITER," ANYWAY?

Believe it or not, by our definition, it's practically anyone who writes music. Songwriting can be a tough process, and there's almost no one for whom brilliant musical and lyrical ideas flow freely whenever they sit down to write—no matter how brilliant a songwriter they might be. Every artist experiences "blocked" periods, and most artists have felt mysteriously "held back," at one time or another, from reaching their full potential. When things get like that, it is always frustrating! So, if you write music of any kind, at some point or another, you'll be what we call a frustrated songwriter.

This book is here to help. If you're the "tortured genius" type of composer—you know that there's a lot of music inside of you, but you chronically struggle with self-doubt, dissatisfaction, nervousness, and other demons—we'll show you a specific course of action that will liberate your creativity in ways you won't believe. If you're creatively less inhibited, but you occasionally suffer from "creative block" (see box), you can use the hundreds of tips and ideas we've collected to work through those periods of frustration. And if you write songs only as a hobby and aren't so emotionally involved in the process, or even if you've never tried writing a song in your life, this book will suggest a way for you to dive into songwriting head-first—and have a ton of fun doing it.

IMMERSION MUSIC METHOD

THERE'S NO MORE rewarding, surprising, and satisfying way to write music than by using our songwriting method, which we call Immersion Music Method (IMM). I first encountered it in 2001, during what was by far the longest dry spell as a songwriter in my life. A good friend of mine, Steven Clark, had been invited to join a composers' group called the Immersion Composition Society, and he enjoyed it so much he asked if he could start his own group for musicians that he knew, including myself. He explained how ICS members write songs and gave me the date of our first meeting, and I started working.

Just a half-hour or so into my first session, I knew something extraordinary was happening. Music just started flowing out of me—and some of it was as good as anything I had ever done. By the time I was finished, some 12 hours later, I realized I had just experienced the most creatively productive day of my life. Although the process was intense, it wasn't especially difficult. It was fun—and it was extremely liberating, because it felt as if all the musical ideas that had been building up inside of me over the previous few years had suddenly exploded out.

We called our group the Immersion Composition Society's "Wig Lodge." Soon, other lodges started springing up. As of this writing, there are songwriter "lodges" all over the U.S. and even in Canada. Hundreds—probably thousands—of cutting-edge songs have been written. ICS members have composed entire operas and requiems during their sessions, and if you know where to look, you can even find IMM-produced music on the shelves at Best Buy.

THE IMM EXPERIENCE

A FUNNY THING happens when you start writing music using our method—particularly when you go "all the way" with it, and form a local songwriter lodge. In addition to producing a much greater quantity of music, people tend to undergo a quantum leap in the *quality* of their music as well. Typically, when someone attends a lodge meeting for the first time, they aren't sure what to expect. When they hear what other experienced IMM songwriters have written, they undergo a kind of shock, and perhaps a bit of intimidation. Almost immediately they want to do a second session to reach deeper into their musical potential—and they do. From one session to the next, their abilities can seem to double, whether it be their songwriting, orchestration, or production skills, or all of the above. (Within the ICS, this sophomore-effort surge has come to be known as the "revenge session.") The spirit of affectionate competition that drives a lodge means that members keep setting the bar higher and higher for each other. It's a very healthy form of peer pressure, and it pushes people to become the best songwriters and musicians that they can possibly be.

Immersion Music Method has literally changed my life and the lives of many other songwriters. So when ICS creator and co-founder Nicholas Dobson approached me about writing a book detailing the method, it was a no-brainer. After all, we had an extended family of ICS members whose brains we could pick, which is exactly what we did. *The Frustrated Songwriter's Handbook* compiles all of the ideas from dozens of IMM composers who, at one time, were frustrated songwriters themselves. We wrote the book because we feel your pain, and because we want to show you the way to the Promised Land of musical creativity.

HOW TO USE THIS BOOK

BASICALLY, THERE ARE two ways to approach IMM songwriting. You can go full-bore and depend on it for most or all of the music you write, have regular all-day IMM sessions, and form or become a member of a songwriter lodge. Or, you can borrow elements from the method, adapt them as you see fit, and casually work on your own. If you decide to immerse yourself in IMM songwriting, this book will guide you step-by-step through the process, tell you what to expect, and suggest what to do with the heap of new music you'll produce as a result. If you'd rather take a more casual approach, you should probably read the book cover-to-cover anyway, as you're bound to pick up bits of wisdom and inspiring nuggets that we've gathered. In particular, Chapter 5, the Compendium, is a grab bag of helpful tips and tricks for generating song ideas and collaborating with others in new, exciting ways, and the Compendium also brims with techniques for overcoming "blocks" and other obstacles. So even if you're only sitting down for an hour or two of messing around with an instrument or a home studio, try leafing though the first part of the Compendium ("Generating Raw Material") and randomly choosing one of the "starts"—that may be all it takes to get your faucet of creativity flowing.

Whichever the case, keep in mind that songwriting doesn't need to be miserable, hard work. Our method is built around making it as fun and playful as possible. You'll find that when you're having a good time and welcoming anything that might happen—whether it's an ecstatic explosion of peak inspiration, or the kind of hilarious, fall-on-your-face failure that will have you and your friends laughing until you gasp for air—the musical ideas *will* flow. That's what this book is all about.

A NOTE ABOUT "RULES"

IN THIS BOOK'S early chapters, we write about how self-imposed and socially reinforced rules can stifle your creativity—but later, we lay out a new list of rules for you to follow. What's up with that? The rules we *do* ask you to follow are for a very specific songwriting process called the 20-Song Game, and the Game's rules are there for a reason. But, as mentioned above, you don't have to follow our method to the letter. If you are adopting a more casual approach, feel free to grab and re-appropriate our techniques any way you want. Even if you are following the IMM system closely, keep in mind that any rules we specify are here to help, not to hinder. You will invariably run into situations where breaking the rules is the right thing to do. You'll get a better idea of when and how to do this as you read through the book. —KC

WHAT IS CREATIVE BLOCK?

IF YOU ARE A songwriter having trouble writing music, and you go to the bookstore looking for an answer, you'll find a lot of books on the general subject of creativity that say you have "creative block." Creative block is a kind of work-related problem originally observed in writers (back then, it was just called "writer's block"). The simplest definition of creative block might go like this: "The inability to make art, even though the artist is technically *able* to, and really *wants* to—leading to suffering on the part of the artist."

Creative block can take the form of dry spells, where the artist doesn't seem to have any ideas, or it can manifest as an inability to "get started." It can also take the form of an inability to "finish anything." Sometimes, creative block is described in terms of the artist hating every idea that they come up with.

Overall, "creative block" generally refers to periods where the artist is "stuck," or believes himself or herself to be "dried up."

WHERE DOES CREATIVE BLOCK COME FROM?

THERE ISN'T ONE answer to that question, but many. There are as many schools of thought relating to analyzing and treating creative block as there are different schools of psychology, itself.

Just to give you a small idea of *how* different . . .

1. A strictly *mental* approach would say that creative block arises from a disorganized work process, and bad mental habits, like over-editing, procrastinating, and setting your expectations too high. Solution: Improve your working habits.

2. An *emotion*-centered approach would argue that creative block arises from a fear of authority, critics, the disapproval of family and friends, or it can arise from a tense relationship with society as a whole. Solution: Work out your feelings.

But where does Immersion Music Method stand on creative block?

THE IMM VIEW ON CREATIVE BLOCK

WHEN YOU ARE blocked, you are at war with your own creative process, and at war with your own motivations and fears. After a while, your block can seem to swell up and fill your entire life, grinding everything to a halt. At times like that, it's easy to find yourself wondering, "Is this problem in my head, or in my heart? Is there something I'm doing wrong, or is there just something wrong with the entire world?"

IMM's answer to those questions is: "Yes."

That is to say, creative block is all of those things. It can be a mental problem, a practical problem, a subconscious problem, and an emotional problem. It can also stem from the stuff *outside* of you: It can be a *social* problem. An artist moves through life and naturally meets a lot of people who say, "Hey, you can't do that!" or, "This kind of art is good, and that kind of art is bad!" Since artists tend to be sensitive people, they can be even more open and susceptible to this kind of negative talk than a "normal" person. In other words, in human society, there have always been these crazy ideas flying around all the time—prohibitive, punitive, *blocked* ways of thinking, just waiting to attach themselves to your brain, and screw you up!

This may sound like bad news, but it isn't. That is to say, it doesn't make creative block any more complicated an adversary. It just means that there are that many more convenient directions, angles, and positions from which to reach, attack, isolate, study, and beat creative block.

Having said all of this, the most ironic thing about the IMM solution is how ridiculously simple it actually is. (See Chapter 1.)

THE BIGGER PICTURE

THE FRUSTRATED SONGWRITER'S HANDBOOK sees creative block as just a small part of a larger problem. More worrisome than the mere, momentary inability to start or finish a song is the loss of the sense of wonder, idealism, and exploration that draws a person to songwriting in the first place. This is a big picture that can include general dissatisfaction, the inability to "break free," isolation, self-sabotage, and "giving up."

The Immersion Composition Society was formed to assist the frustrated songwriter on as many levels as possible. That's why we hesitate to refer to our book as a method merely for beating creative block. While IMM is most definitely a system for doing that, it also overflows with radical but simple ideas for building a musical support community—ways that musicians can band together and help each other. —ND

ACKNOWLEDGMENTS

I'D LIKE TO thank David Cooper, for his design of the Immersion Composition Society crest. I'd like to thank 'Thbun, for mentorship, beans, and for making everything possible (and for not kicking me out). I want to thank my family. Also, John Queen, who is part of my family. So is Nat Hawkes. I thank the lodges of the Immersion Composition Society: Origin Lodge, Wig Lodge, Neptune Lodge, New Lodge, Bullet Lodge, X-ray Lodge, Thelemic Lodge, Capsicum Lodge, Urchin Lodge, Red Curtain Lodge, Glamour Lodge, Limestone Lodge, Veronica Lodge, Zero Lodge, Black Lodge, Kraken Lodge, and Econo Lodge. Also, the infamous "No Nerds Lodge," who proclaimed it their solemn duty to beat up everyone in the ICS. I'd like to thank SGM for wearing a lot of greasepaint and emitting loud crunching noises. Thanks to the Oakland family of musicians and artists that has been, well, a family to me. Thanks to Bethel for the coolest thing anyone has ever done for me. I'd like to thank Class 13, Class 14, and the staff at Ex'pression. I'd like to thank Lianne Mueller. I thank Steven Clark, for getting the idea to call these things "lodges." I'd like to thank Kai Esbensen for furry hats with horns on them, and the Mall of America. I'd like to thank Christo. I'd like to thank Mick for showing up at my house randomly, and entertaining me while I was writing. I'd like to thank all of the friendly faces at work. I want to thank Kurt Vonnegut Jr., for his writings on the necessity of artificial extended families. I want to thank the mainstream, for knowing how to communicate. I'd like to thank the avant garde, for having something to communicate in the first place. Be friends, please.

—NICHOLAS DOBSON

I WOULD LIKE to thank the entire Immersion Composition Society, and everyone who gives Immersion Music Method a shot. I hope IMM changes your lives as much as it has mine.

—KARL CORYAT

CHAPTER ONE

The Hamster Wheel

Catch-22: A problematic situation for which the only solution is denied by a circumstance inherent in the problem.

—Webster's Collegiate Dictionary

WHEN YOU ARE a frustrated songwriter, it isn't enough just to write a song. Anyone can do that! *You* want it to sound a certain way. If it doesn't end up that way, you don't want to have written it in the first place.

Ideally, your song should be so good, a person listening to it would see a geometric vision of infinity, lose muscular control, and collapse to the ground like a sack of rivets.

Otherwise, what's the point?

SOMETIMES, A SONGWRITER'S self-imposed rules and expectations can build up and get really complicated. You might spend weeks or months (or even years) in songwriter purgatory, waiting—but not sure what exactly it is that you're waiting for. The right moment? A special feeling? For Jupiter to ascend into Pisces? And this time you spend stuck in the middle of a song, unable to get started, or unable to "cut loose"—it's not restful, even when you aren't really doing anything. A feeling of unfinished business hangs over everything, like a curse.

In your mind, you are a songwriter, and you are working. But in fact, in the real world, nothing is happening. It's almost like being a hamster on an exercise wheel, and the wheel is attached to a cage—but this cage is in your mind, where you can't see it.

Meanwhile, your friends grab you by the shoulders and shake you around, saying, "Snap out of it! You are brilliant! Why are you acting like this? Just write the flipping song!"

IRONICALLY, ONE THING that doesn't help is all of the advice that people give you. Everyone you meet is an expert! A guy at the bus stop says, "It sounds like you're afraid of success, buddy. Don't be!" You get on the bus, and a girl in a Bauhaus T-shirt leans over and says, "I overheard you back there. Just remember, whatever you do, don't sell out!"

A week later finds you pacing your basement apartment, clutching a cigarette that went out three days ago, muttering, "Let's see … don't be afraid of success … don't sell out … don't be afraid of success. Ummmm . . . ."

So you say to yourself, "Those were phony experts, anyway. What was I thinking? I'll ask some real experts!"

"You don't have to do or be anything." —Therapist

"With great power comes great responsibility." —A musician friend

"Resolve your conflicts." —A self-help book you read

"Conflict is the essence of interest." —A college writing teacher

ADVICE TO HELP! Rules to help! And yet, the more little rules you create for yourself, and the more bits of advice you pick up from everywhere, the more they weigh you down. They fight each other. They contradict each other. They seem to demand that you move in three directions at once. Before long, you are running laps in your head all day, trying in vain to get somewhere, anywhere, and your life is beginning to resemble some sort of skewed, alternate universe that you can't escape—a place where something is always about to happen, but nothing ever does.

A feeling not unlike being a hamster on an exercise wheel.

WHEN YOU ARE a frustrated songwriter, this is how everything works. Everything goes around and around and around. Your mind is always trying to dart ahead and do things before you do them. You can feel judged and scrutinized—even though the opinionated friend you recently had over left an hour ago—and you always feel like you are working, when actually you haven't started working, yet.

Nothing is clear, and nothing is simple. Nobody can help you, and you can't help yourself. Every decision grows and multiplies into its own enormous subject. Every rule is something you aren't supposed to do, and when you add them all up, they tell you to do nothing.

So, is *The Frustrated Songwriter's Handbook* going to help you sort out these feelings? Are we going to tell you how to navigate the rule-maze and reach an elegant solution, where all of this mental noise resolves into beautiful clarity? Well, actually, no. The solution goes more like this:

No more thinking for you!

AN OVERVIEW OF IMMERSION MUSIC METHOD (IMM)

WHEN YOU ARE a "blocked" songwriter, it can feel like there is all of this complicated stuff that you have to think about, important feelings that you have to process, and a special "mood" that has to arrive, before you actually get to *make music*. Immersion Music Method is a system of songwriting techniques—or, as we call them, games—designed to cut through this false dilemma, like a sword through the Gordian Knot.[1] IMM is not about figuring things out,

---

1. According to ancient Greek legend, there was an elaborate knot, rumored to be unsolvable, tied to an ox cart near the temple of Zeus in the city of Gordion. An oracle had once said that the man who solved the knot would go on to rule Asia. After innumerable visitors failed to solve the knot over the years, Alexander the Great showed up one day and solved it—by slashing through the knot with his sword. Complicated problem, simple solution!

sorting through your feelings, "consulting the muse," or understanding how the mind works. IMM is about making things happen.

These are games that move *fast*. The goal is to write as much music as humanly possible in a set amount of time, and the game rules leave no time for analysis. The player enters a state of total creative overdrive, where all rules and expectations fly out the window. There's no time to *understand* or *control* anything, the clock is ticking, and your reward is right there, waiting at the end of the day. Motivation wells up from nowhere, and "being blocked" simply ceases to be an option.

Afterward, when you are sorting through your pile of new songs, you will likely find yourself wondering: How did I do that? Did I really make all of these songs? Do I really get to *keep them?*

These games can be played alone, or with a musical friend. They can also be played with a band, to brainstorm up new material, or with fellow students in a conservatory or recording school. For the *total* IMM experience, may we suggest getting on the phone, calling every musician in your area you have ever wanted to spend more time with, and getting together a local IMM game community (see Chapter 4, The Songwriter Lodge). If you thought D&D was a fun way to spend time in a crowded basement . . . .

Immersion Music Method is a simple solution to a complicated problem. No special skills or technical expertise are required. Even if you are planning to take the "home recording" path of IMM, it *still* doesn't matter. You can start on a microcassette recorder and a kazoo, if you want! This dynamic (and highly portable) home recording setup will cost you about $20 at the corner drug store.

IMM also requires very little mental preparation. You don't have to "grow as a person" or achieve "emotional balance" to use this method. And thank God for that! We songwriters need all of that dark, sexy, mysterious conflict to write our songs with, don't you think? By that reasoning, as far as Immersion Music Method is concerned, you can go ahead and *stay conflicted*. Don't bother trying to work things out. Don't seek clarity. Don't find inner peace. Don't problem-solve. Don't try to hold everything together. Don't try to figure out what it all means. Let it *all* crash down! Get lost! Lose track! Let it slide!

This book will open the cage door for you. You will be free to move out into the world, and begin, in deadly earnest, to write a whole lot of songs.

It's time to step off the hamster wheel.

NICHOLAS'S STORY, PART 1
Discovering the 20-Song Game

WHEN I WAS 11 years old, being a songwriter was a very simple proposition. It worked like this: I would sit down and play piano, and I would keep doing that until someone told me to stop.

When I played piano, I was in a

Nicholas

different, better place. I felt like I was exploring magical woods, and these woods were the first thing in my life that truly belonged to me. I wrote songs just to see where they would go, for the joy of it.

After a while, I started to get the idea that when I grew up, I would be a famous musician. This was my 11-year-old idea of how one becomes a professional musician:

1. I would write songs that everyone really liked, and they'd think I was a super-fantastic guy.

2. Then, a mysterious organization would give me money and put me in a cool house that they paid for, because they had realized I was a genius.

Now *that* was a good plan.

_____

ABOUT 16 YEARS later, working in a copy shop in Santa Rosa, California, I realized that my plan had gotten lost somewhere.

Is this what being a grown-up musician was like?

Somewhere between age 11 and the present time, songwriting had ceased to be a form of play and escape. Somehow, it had turned into *work* … maybe something worse than that. It was almost as if songwriting had become a form of *madness*. When I sat down with a guitar and tried to work on something, I met so much resistance in my mind that it was like trying to pedal a bicycle home with a howling headwind pushing me in the opposite direction.

I had the worst case of creative block imaginable.

Sometimes I'd get lucky—my paralysis would break, and I'd actually get started on a song. I'd spend four or five years agonizing over a long, winding opus, trying to fulfill all of my internal rules, trying to say *everything at once*, and trying my best to shake off the irrational feeling that somewhere, a shadowy authority figure, or a giant crowd of people, or a disapproving friend was listening in, monitoring and weighing my every musical idea, and finding it lacking.

A lot of the time, when I was done, I'd realize that this opus of mine was a big, timid failure—a song in which I had concealed everything about myself that someone might not like, written to offend no one, and I'd throw the song away without playing it for anyone. Or, if by some miracle I actually liked my new song, I'd often subconsciously contrive some elaborate way of ensuring that nobody ever heard it. For example, I might decide that my new song was part of a *trilogy*, write the rest of the trilogy, and then throw away the entire trilogy.

My brain was messed up!

SO, IF THERE was an answer, it wasn't *in my head*, right? But when I turned my attention outward and looked to the members of my music community for help, I didn't find answers there, either.

I found more mental noise, instead.

There is so much myth and superstition, and so much bitter politics, among musicians. It seemed like every time a musical friend of mine opened his mouth, a crazy belief would tumble out, or a toxic diatribe about a music-industry conspiracy keeping us all down, or a biting criticism of someone else's band, or yet *another* rule, like, "No guitar solos."

As I listened to all of this negative talk, I would feel my confusion and paralysis get a little worse. Were even some of my friends, unwittingly, holding me back?

Was my creative block in my head, or in my life?

Either way, I was all out of ideas.

Nobody could help me, and I couldn't help myself.

━━━━━━━━━━━━━━━━━━━━

BUT THEN, TWO lucky things happened:

1. I met Michael Mellender, a warped misanthrope with a mad scientist's laugh, who could play about 13 different instruments. And the music! Recorded in his bedroom, it was an astonishing mixture of cartoon music, Russian folk, junk percussion, old horror-movie scores, eerie sonics, and big, heavy guitars. In short, his were songs that made you want to quit your job, go live in a spooky castle, and conduct evil experiments, punctuating every sentence with a flash of lightning.

For the first time in my life, I had found a true *peer*—an exact equal in all things musical, who drove me to better myself.

It wasn't long before we were sending each other 20 e-mails a day, and having long, sprawling conversations about music. As it turned out, we wanted exactly the same thing.

We wanted to throw everything away, and start over.

We talked about forming a new kind of band, or a music club. We talked about *actually making* all of that "totally crazy and amazing" music we had always planned to make. We wanted a new life in music, one that was more like the musician life we had imagined as kids—something closer to the life of a mad scientist, or a composer in a period film, hunched over his piano all day, scribbling by the light of a solitary candle.

Isn't that how it's supposed to be?

2. Around the same time, I moved to Oakland and enrolled in the digital graphic-design program at the Ex'pression Center for New Media in Emeryville (now known as Ex'pression College for Digital Arts; www.xnewmedia.com). At the time, the Ex'pression curriculum was based on *total immersion*, a once-experimental branch of education that taps into

the emergency powers of the human mind. These are the same powers that, in many documented cases, have allowed a person lost in an unfamiliar country to become a nearly fluent speaker of the native language in a matter of months.

By thrusting a student into a similar pressure-learning situation, the Ex'pression Center's methods essentially *forced* that student to absorb four years' worth of stuff in about a year and a half.[2] You had to constantly exceed what you had formerly thought you were physically capable of—on a daily basis—just to make it through. A lot of people dropped out of the Ex'pression Center after experiencing just two weeks of the curriculum.

The pace was frantic! The workload diabolical!

In one class, I was split off into a lab group with four other guys, and we were forced to write and record a pretend radio play, and then create a student film, in a few short days, each. For that entire class, I had felt socially awkward with my lab-mates. I felt like I had started off on the wrong foot, and now, more than anything, I had gotten the idea in my head that I wanted to impress those four guys. I wanted to break the ice! So, I offered to write some music for the movie, and they accepted. I had a couple days to do it. I went home, set up my gear, started working, and . . .

My creative block disappeared.

———————————————————————

2. The Ex'pression curriculum has undergone a lot of changes over time, and we hear the curriculum is less time-compressed than it once was. But the general idea remains that of immersing the mind in digital media, and learning a whole lot of stuff.

OF COURSE I didn't notice, at the time, that my creative block had been temporarily turned off. I was too busy to think about stuff like that! I had one weekend in which to make something just impressive enough to impress those four guys. What could be simpler?

My mind focused to a white-hot point. I was filled with an excitement I hadn't felt since I was 11 years old. The entire weekend flew by like a tornado.

When the dust cleared, I was left holding a CD filled with music, feeling like a pinball that has just emerged from the far end of a pinball machine. I took this music to the guys in my lab, and their eyes popped out of their heads. It was a real ice-breaker!

My eyes popped out of my head, too, because it was the best music I had ever made in my entire life.

———————————————

THAT WAS WHEN I really started to puzzle over recent events. This thing that had happened flew in the face of everything I had ever believed about inspiration and creativity.

For years I had been a creatively blocked basket-case, and I had been treating it like a mental problem. I had analyzed it from every angle. I had read books. I had tried to think it through. I had tried to have a really good attitude. Nothing had helped.

Some of the musicians around me spoke about creativity and inspiration as a spiritual force, and as silly as this sounds, I had appealed to this force in every way I could think of. I had tried to maintain artistic integrity. I had looked for small signs. I had knocked on wood. I had even found myself stepping over the cracks in the pavement, from time to time. That hadn't helped, either.

But, make one small tweak in my *situation*, and suddenly there's no problem! Give me an impossible deadline, zero quality expectations, and the promise of a small, captive audience, and I become the musical version of the Tasmanian Devil!

It was a completely new world. There was such a thing as a creative-block-proof situation. Were there more of those situations where that one had come from? Could a person, maybe … make their own?

I was starting to get ideas. Not just ideas about creative block, but ideas about cutting loose in general. Ideas about "immersion." Ideas about my and Michael's weekend music club. Ideas about throwing it all away and starting over.

A FEW DAYS later, I sent Michael an e-mail. The message contained the rules for a musical game that I had just thought up, and I asked him if he wanted to play.

He immediately said YES.

It was to be a "composer duel" that would take place over the course of one day.

THE RULES: (1) On the day of the duel, each of us would wake up, in his separate house, and try to write and record 20 new songs. (2) Whoever ended up having more songs at the end of the day "won." If both of us got 20, it was a tie. (3) These songs would contain no pre-written material. (4) They could be any length, and it didn't matter what they sounded like.

(5) At the end of the day, one of us would drive over to the other person's house, and together, we would have a party, and listen to the music we had made.

AS FAR AS I could tell, I had just thought up a game that would make creative block impossible.

PART 2

I WOKE UP at 6:30 in the morning, and was instantly, totally awake. By the time my feet hit the floor, I already knew that this was a day I had been waiting for my entire life. I leaped out of bed and virtually sprinted into the kitchen. After a moment of deliberation, I decided against calling Michael at this hour. Instead, I brewed a strong pot of coffee, had ice cream and red spicy Cheetos for breakfast, took my guitar out of its case, set up a microphone, fired up my keyboard, jumped up and down with impatience as my computer started up, sat down, and . . .

went utterly berserk.

TWO HOURS LATER, when my roommate Nat woke up, I had already written: (1) a delicate orchestral piece with a meandering melody, sounding like a cross between Dead Can Dance and Frank Zappa; (2) three extremely short, fast, and complicated death metal songs in MIDI format; (3) the soundtrack to an action sequence in a fake movie, involving mariachi music and machine-gun fire, and then a helicopter rescue, but then the hero gets shot in the back, and the whole things ends in a quote of "La Cucaracha" played really slow, in a minor key.

I threw open my bedroom door as Nat shuffled into the kitchen (our bedrooms opened to the kitchen) and played the action sequence to him. He looked really sleepy, and laughed a lot. I laughed, too, because I was having so much fun. Then I closed the door again.

Ten minutes later I opened the door to the kitchen with a flourish, and played him another song I had made, and we both laughed again.

Then the phone rang. I picked it up, and it was Michael Mellender, screaming in my ear. He was very excited about the way his session was going (but it should be noted that, for him, this is a normal way to say hello). I said, "I've got five songs! What have you got, you slimy, god-forsaken maggot?"

He said, "Foolish pig-dog! I have exceeded your number by no less than three!"

And I said, "Dammit!"

I played him one of my songs over the phone, and he played me one of his songs. All I could hear was a distorted clattering sound (but it should be noted that, for him, this is a normal way to write music). Throughout the day we would call each other and elaborately insult each other, like two noblemen dueling with swords, and demand to know how many songs the other guy had.

A COUPLE OF hours later, I had a paradigm-altering experience that I now consider totally essential to making music. (See Chapter 5, Steamrolling, page 97.) I started writing a song, and suddenly I realized that it was going very well, and that it sounded "beautiful" and "deep." I thought, This might end up being one of my "real" songs! All I had to do was write an appropriately beautiful and deep chorus. Then I thought about all of the people who might someday listen to my song, and this had the immediate effect of grinding my songwriting process to a halt.

I was stuck.

I stared blankly at my computer screen for 15 minutes, completely paralyzed. I listened to what I had so far of the song, again and again, but for the life of me I couldn't figure out what should go next. I scratched my head and twiddled my thumbs.

Then, I had a sudden, wonderful epiphany: I want to write a chorus that will impress all of the listeners in the world, but I don't know how. The more people I try to please at the same time, the more bogged down everything gets. And, besides, how would I know what all of the listeners in the world want?

But I do know how to make Michael Mellender laugh.

Destroy the song! Blast it to pieces! Trample on it! Make it *funny!* The look on Michael's face, when he hears this, is plenty to look forward to, for me, today. When today is over, I'll have the rest of my life to fix this stupid song and make it sound all "deep" again.

So, I did just that. I wrote the most jarring, inappropriate chorus imaginable (it sounded a bit like the shower-scene music from *Psycho*) and moved on to the next song.

Later, I would realize that I hadn't destroyed the song at all. In fact, it was my best song that day. I would also realize something else, something even more important: When you are in the process of writing a song, it doesn't really matter what you are thinking, what your "intentions" are, or where you start. You don't have to be thinking deep thoughts, or maintaining artistic integrity, or trying to "get inspired." If you put in enough hours, and you enjoy yourself, and you're willing to try anything, you will get lucky and write something amazing, and it will be yours forever.

So, play, and be free!

———————————

BY THE END of the day there were cords and gear tangling and zig-zagging all over my room, and the floor was littered with empty, destroyed junk-food packages. My left eye was twitching, and my session had devolved into a quest to find out what is the most annoying noise a person can make with their mouth.

Then Michael was knocking on the door. He had a cassette tape with his session on it, a six-pack, and more junk food. He stomped around my living room, said a bunch of stuff I don't remember, and then collapsed on my couch. He said something along the lines of, "I want to do this every day, and never leave my house."

I said, "Me, too."

The listening party was yet another revelation. As might be expected, the music that we had collected throughout the day was filled with moments of sublime ridiculousness, hilariously awful noise, and things that people do not normally say out loud. We played this jokey filler material over and over, laughing until we could barely breathe.

But there was something else.

THERE WERE ALSO sweetly beautiful songs. They had the quality of a childhood dream that you had almost forgotten—but now this dream was on a cassette tape, and it could be played for people.

There were also songs that, for some reason, sounded like they had been methodically constructed and *thought out*, even though, in reality, they had been written in about seven minutes. Other songs had a quality of flying apart into total chaos, and then unexpectedly snapping into formation at a later point, like a flock of birds—while still others seemed to somehow do both at the same time, inhabiting a tantalizing gray area between orchestration and improvisation.

It was as if our entire lives as musicians had been a farce, and we had been hiding the brightest, best parts of ourselves behind cautious, two-dimensional, apologetic musical personas. We had spent our entire lives talking about this crazy, adventurous music that we were going to make someday, and we had never allowed ourselves to do it. But that farce had ended, and those better, brighter parts were being let out. We felt like we could literally do anything.

We were completely addicted. From then on, we were going to do this every other Saturday.

CHAPTER TWO

The 20-Song Game

*"If a fool persisted in his folly,
he would become wise."*

—William Blake

ASK YOURSELF THIS: What is the largest number of songs you've ever written in one day? One, two at most?

Now ask yourself this: What is the *fastest* you've ever written a song? If you're like most songwriters, you've come up with entire songs—including lyrics—in just an hour or two of frenzied inspiration. Maybe it has taken even less time than that; many musicians speak of coming up with song ideas almost instantly, the song seeming to "write itself" as it was played and/or sung for the first time. Often, these types of songs end up being the writer's favorites, flowing as they did from the heart straight onto the manuscript paper or tape deck.

That's *inspiration*, right?

When inspiration strikes, things happen fast—and suddenly, writing a song becomes much easier than it is when you aren't so inspired.

NOW, WHAT WOULD happen if you tried to *make* that type of frenzied inspiration happen, by forcing yourself to write a song very quickly—almost instantly, say—whether you felt "inspired" or not? Well, you might very well come up with a big pile of dog crap. But how about if you tried to write a *bunch* of songs very quickly, almost instantly? Would that simply result in a bunch of big piles of dog crap?

Not likely. Surely, some of the piles will be less crappy than others. Some of them might actually be good.

One or two might be really, *really* good.

THE HEART OF IMMERSION Music Method is the "20-Song Game," and it's the key to salvation for frustrated songwriters everywhere.

A lot of the magic of the Game lies in the way it uses and directs our fears and motivations, in a sense turning our creative block inside out, so that it stops pushing against us, and begins, instead, to push us forward.

HOW TO PLAY

HERE'S HOW THE Game works: Set aside a day when you have no appointments or obligations, and on that day, try to write 20 new songs. It's as simple as that. You don't think you could ever write 20 songs in one day? Have you ever tried it? It actually isn't as impossible as it sounds.

Mind you, we didn't say you that these songs had to be intricately worked out, or for that matter, particularly coherent. As you have no doubt picked up already, this isn't about trying to write 20 *good* songs. That, in fact, would be difficult or impossible.

But, proud songwriter that you are, you may find every cell in your body violently resisting the idea of writing a less-than-great song, or of continuing to work on a song that you knew was sub-par from the start.

Get over it!

RULES OF THE 20-SONG GAME

1. The Game is played in a session that is at least 12 hours long—one continuous time block.

2. The goal is to write 20 *completely new* songs in one day.

3. These songs are to be written from scratch, without incorporating any of your own pre-written material—that is to say, none of the actual writing of notes, rhythms, or lyrics can be done on an earlier date. However, loose conceptual things like song titles, arrangement ideas, descriptions, genres, etc., *can* be sketched out in advance. (See Chapter 5 for more details on "Pre-arranging.")

4. If you are the kind of songwriter who incorporates samples, quotes of other music, or found text into your songs, feel free to keep making music the way you normally do. The "no pre-written material" rule applies only to *your* material. It's there to keep you moving forward and generating new ideas, not to cramp your style!

5. During the session, don't engage in any tasks except writing music. That's why it's *Immersion* Music—don't check your e-mail, don't pay your bills, and don't sort your laundry. Immerse yourself in the process!

6. If you get stuck, just play or sing *anything*. It doesn't matter! Don't get mired down trying to come up with the perfect part or lyric—save that for another time.

7. Avoid doing second takes if you're recording. Record one take and move on.

8. It's okay if you don't reach the 20-song goal, as long as you actually tried. Five or ten songs can make up a very productive session.

9. When multiple people play the Game (which we heartily recommend), the Game starts with the players splitting up. Each player, individually, writes as many songs as they can. At the end of the day, the players come together for a meeting, where they share their results (see Chapter 4, The Songwriter Lodge).

SONGWRITING IN ZERO GRAVITY

ACCORDING TO SOME motivational literature, artists (and people in general) hold themselves back because of a subconscious "fear of success." *The Frustrated Songwriter's Handbook* would like to go out on a limb and submit a different theory: When songwriters hold themselves back, it's not success—or even failure—that they necessarily fear. It's that if they fail as a songwriter and, say, write a very awful song, that something *really bad* might happen. For example, you might write an incredibly bad song, and everyone in the world might point and laugh at you. Or, maybe you'd fail commercially, and not have any money, and get evicted around wintertime, and have to go sleep under a bridge, and be mauled to death by a roving pack of raccoons.

It's neither success that we fear nor, for that matter, even *failure* itself. If there were no consequences to failure—if nothing bad happened to you—it wouldn't really be a very big deal to fail, would it? Consider this: Let's say you are walking a tightrope, and that tightrope is two feet off the ground. If you lose your balance and fall off, that's failure, isn't it? But who cares! You chuckle and get back on. However, move that rope up a few hundred feet, and maybe string it between two skyscrapers, and, hey, what do you know? Keeping your balance suddenly becomes a matter of some concern! It is the potentially dire *consequences* of failure that we fear.

Keeping that in mind, when a frustrated songwriter plays the 20-Song Game, they are stepping into a situation that is so psychologically potent, it's almost magical. Why? Because, among many other things, the 20-Song Game is a *consequence-free zone.*

In a very real sense, it's pretty much ridiculous to expect anything useful to come out of a one-day, 20-song writing spree. It's not a very *serious* proposition, is it? So, who cares if you lose? Who cares what the songs sound like? You made 20 of these bloody things! How good are they supposed to sound? In other words, failure doesn't mean much under the circumstances. Stepping into the 20-Song Game, it might be said, you step into not only a zone free of consequences, but a zone that is similarly free of *expectations.*

And that is why you are free to do anything you want.

It is a creative situation that finds its best analogy in one of those huge, inflatable castles that you find in county fairs, the ones that are so fun to jump around in when you are a kid. You can do anything you want. Anything! You can fall on your face, fall backwards with nobody there to catch you, or leap directly onto your head if you want to. You just bounce off!

It is completely astonishing what happens to a person, and what they become capable of, when they know that they can't get hurt, when nothing *counts*, and they're just *messing around*. Have you ever found yourself, maybe, executing an effortless backflip on a trampoline, when you would never attempt such a maneuver on the ground? Ever leapt off a rooftop into a backyard swimming pool? Same basic principle—there's this maneuver that normally you wouldn't be able to do, but you now can do it, because that trampoline, or that swimming pool, is there to catch you.

This is how it feels to know that the music you are writing isn't "real" music, but *play* music. Music written just to see where it goes, for the joy of it.

Members of the Immersion Composition Society have pulled off startling and amazing feats under the "zero-gravity" creativity conditions of the 20-Song Game. They might suddenly *learn* to play an instrument passably well that they could barely play before, or they might suddenly discover a new singing voice that they didn't know they had in them, or they might suddenly be able to do a perfect impression of some style of music they've never played before.

"GAME PRESSURE"

THIS IS NOT to say that the 20-Song Game is without *pressure*. In fact, the pressure can at times be almost unbearably intense. As ICS member Matt Lebofsky (Origin Lodge, Oakland, California) puts it, "All I know is that if the whole recording day goes by without me either jumping up and down in primal excitement or sobbing uncontrollably, then it wasn't a good session."

Have you ever felt the real world recede into the back of your mind as you focused all of your energy on, say, winning a round of Scrabble? Or, have you ever been so intent on beating a friend at one-on-one basketball that it felt like winning was the most important thing in the world? People can get pretty intense about games! That is why the 20-Song Game has such an intense power to push you along as a songwriter, feeding you energy and momentum and determination throughout your session.

WHY 20 SONGS?

IN A CONVENTIONAL songwriting session, if you start by coming up with some chord changes on guitar, and those first three or four chords don't knock you out, you can get discouraged—fast. If you start with a drum-machine beat, you might convince yourself that the song sucks before you so much as touch another instrument. If you start with a lyric, you might be so self-conscious—even though there's nobody else in the room—that you can't get past the first line. *Nobody is going to want to hear these words! "I want you baby, you turn me on like a porch light, baby"? I'm pathetic!*

Here's the problem: No matter how skilled or unskilled a songwriter you may be, you really have *no idea* how a song is going to turn out until you've finished writing it. If you crumple up the page after writing just one line, you've given up without even giving the song a chance. Who knows where that "porch light" lyric was headed? Maybe, if you had continued, you would have started to hit your stride by the end of the second verse; then you might have gone back and revised verse 1. Also, remember that some of the greatest songs ever written don't have brilliant lyrics. They're classics because of something else about them: the groove, a bass-line hook, whatever. But what would have happened if their composers had given up after the first line or two? Those now-classic songs never would have seen the light of day.

When you're playing the 20-Song Game, you don't have the luxury of judging a song as it's starting to take shape. Since you've given yourself the extreme goal of writing so many songs, there's no time to read or listen back to what you've written and say, "Pretty good," or "Holy hell!" You just have to keep going. Your session will include some songs that didn't "work out." That's a given; it always happens. *Always!* After the session is over, you'll have all the time in the world to decide which songs worked and which didn't—but while you're writing, just plow ahead and don't look back.

WHAT TO EXPECT

IN ACTUALITY, IT'S pretty rare to reach the 20-song goal. But the goal is an important one, a goal to always keep in mind, which is why it's called the 20-Song Game even if you write only eight songs. After playing the Game many times, and perhaps after you've reached 20 a few times, you'll likely find a comfortable average number of songs that you normally produce. But always shooting for 20 in earnest keeps you in the proper mindset and keeps

ON BREAKING THE RULES

WHILE THE VOLUME-focused rules of the 20-Song Game caution you against getting hung up on quality, every once in a while during a session, you might find yourself tweaking out on a detail or two—in other words, "breaking the rules." Don't worry, it's totally normal! IMM isn't an *exact science*, where all operations happen in a perfect vacuum. And remember, the rules of the 20-Song Game are here to help, not to hinder. This is about writing a lot of music, and being free, not beating yourself up because you got a little obsessed somewhere in your session and spent (gasp!) *an hour and 20 minutes* on one song. These rules are not guidelines for life, or some voice telling you how to think. They are tools, designed to help you write as much music as possible.

That said, when you find yourself tempted to fixate on quality while playing the 20-Song Game, our advice is: Fight it every inch of the way! Keep a cautious eye on that quality-obsession demon. Every time you give in to the urge to zoom in and freak out over a small detail, you run a good chance of lapsing into your old, more conventional (read: frustrated) songwriting mentality, where everything is slow and painful. This can bog down your entire songwriting session!

you moving forward. Also, generally, the more songs you come up with, the more *good* songs you'll come up with. If you write 20, almost certainly one or two—if not a lot more—will be what you would ordinarily call "inspired."

Of course, even if you're a one-in-a-million talent, you aren't likely to finish with 20 fully arranged and developed songs. Most or all of them will be just ideas—maybe just a chorus, or

THE THREE-MINUTE BURN

FOR SOME PEOPLE, being able to summon a free creative flow of any kind—good or bad—is an alien prospect. It's not something we do in our day-to-day life. Even in a freewheeling conversation with a close friend, we're constantly editing ourselves, as one part of our mind (Freudians call it the "superego") says "no" to ideas coming from another part (the "id").

The 20-Song Game is all about free creative flow. You need to be able to make it happen, or Immersion Music simply will not occur. Here's an easy exercise that will help.

Take a sheet of notebook paper. At the end of this exercise, you will be burning this sheet of paper—keep that in mind. Now, for three minutes, do nothing but write down phrases and sentences as soon as they come to you, and write as fast as you can. (This is commonly called "stream of consciousness" writing.) Do not stop; do not pause. Just write anything. The goal is to fill up as much of the page as you can in that three minutes. Your words don't have to be comprehensible, or politically correct, or anything else. *Just write anything*.

When the three minutes are over, glance over what you've written. If you see something interesting—maybe a cool concept or a potential title for a future song—copy it down somewhere else.

a verse and chorus with a melody but no words. That's okay.[1] The important thing is that each song be *something*—"good" or "bad," it doesn't matter. At the end of the day there will be

---

1. As we say in the Immersion Composition Society, "If it has a track number, it's a song." In other words, it's enough of a song that you can move on to something else, if necessary.

Then burn the sheet of paper. Nobody will ever know what you wrote.

Even for someone who's experienced at IMM, or who doesn't have a problem letting go of their self-editing tendencies, this exercise is a good way to get in the proper mindset for the 20-Song Game. A variation is called *freewriting*; the concept is similar, but here the idea is to write about a particular topic and maintain a certain minimum focus. Freewriting is a great way to come up with rough song lyrics fast, so it can be a powerful technique to use when you're actually playing the 20-Song Game.

a pile of songs, each conveying a mood or idea—each a song that wasn't there before. That is what matters. Of course, if one of those songs ends up being a "keeper," there should be enough substance there to build on, should you choose to polish it up later (see Chapter 6).

The 20-Song Game can be an emotional rollercoaster. One moment you're on top of the world; you can't believe how well things are going. Move on to another song, though, and you're in agony; you're hating life, and you can't believe that you're coming up with this piece of rotting tripe. Just remember: This is a *game!* Games are supposed to be fun! The songs that are "failures," or their number, are no reflection on your talent. The more you can loosen up your attitudes about failure—or even better, *celebrate* the failures—the more pure your Game experience will be, and you'll be in a better frame of mind to come up with other, more successful ideas.

WORK STYLES: SONG-BY-SONG VS. ASSEMBLY-LINE

THERE ARE TWO basic ways to approach the 20-Song Game. Some people prefer starting the first song, finishing it, then going to song No. 2 and finishing that one, etc. The advantage is that once you're ready to move on, you know you've got a song in the can, and when you reach that last song, your work is done.

However, recording musicians may find it much easier to reach the 20-song goal with an "assembly line" approach, where (for example) you lay down 20 drum grooves, then go back and lay down a bass line for each drum groove, and so on. You can record a lot of music very fast this way. The downside is that the songs will tend to have similar arrangements, and most of them will have the same genesis (a bass-and-drums groove in the above example), which may limit your creations' diversity. Also, when you're laying down one instrumental part, you may hear an idea for another instrument that you aren't ready to record yet—and you risk forgetting your idea by the time you come back to that song.

It's often good to combine these approaches. If you have an idea to develop the song you're currently working on, keep going. If not, move on to the next one and come back to it later.

CHAPTER THREE

The Day Session

"Exterminate all rational thought."

—William S. Burroughs

WHEN MENTAL OBSTACLES get in the way of your songwriting, or you feel held back somehow from achieving a musical goal, the IMM solution is: Turn it into a game! If you want it to be really fun, turn it into a game you can play with your friends. In IMM, most games take place over the course of a day. You wake up, and you have until the day is over to make as much music as you can. This 12-hour time block is called a "Day Session."

The Day Session is one of the three cornerstone concepts of Immersion Music Method (along with the 20-Song Game and the Songwriter Lodge). It is astonishing what a simple 12-hour deadline can do to the mind of a frustrated songwriter. Attitudes shift, and priorities alter.

Suddenly, that songwriter remembers what "today" is for.

Okay. So you'd like to try your hand at playing the 20-Song Game. Do you just plunge in and go for it?

Yes, and no. Not surprisingly, "plunging in" is exactly what you need to do for any "immersive" activity. But Immersion Music Method seems to go more smoothly and effortlessly with a bit of preparation before, and some guidelines during, each Day Session.

SCHEDULING

NATURALLY, TRY TO schedule your Day Session when you'll actually be able to dedicate your full attention to music. During the block of time you're setting aside, you should have no actual appointments, and preferably there should be nothing that needs to get done (other than write songs, of course), no matter how trivial.

Your Day Session should consist of a single 12-hour block of time. If your lifestyle makes this difficult, hold out for a while and see if a free 12-hour block comes up in your schedule. The 20-Song Game is about writing 20 songs in a day, right? In the Immersion Composition Society, that has always been the rule—not that some of our busier members haven't occasionally broken that rule. Yes, if there is no other way for you to try IMM for the first time than to bend the 12-hour rule—breaking your session down into, say, two six-hour blocks—have at it. Give IMM a try! But keep in mind that if you never get around to trying the real thing, you might be sort of missing the point of the Day Session, not to mention missing some amazing benefits. Really good things tend to happen toward the end of grueling 12-hour music sessions, and anything that causes your mind to shift focus will take your focus off music—and in our method, that isn't good.

MENTAL DETOX

IT DEPENDS ON personality, but even many veteran members of the Immersion Composition Society have to work to get into, and stay in, the proper mindset for playing the Game. The "traditional," self-editing, quality-seeking songwriter mindset may be burned into your psyche, almost like part of your genetic code—particularly if you've been writing songs for a long time. A big part of preparing for a Day Session involves unlearning these concepts. Think of it as a kind of deprogramming—like what cult followers go through after they've been rescued: You have been *brainwashed* into thinking that writing music must be a labored and methodical process, one driven by constant analysis and evaluation, one in which you're helpless and powerless to the whim of the music-writing gods. Unlearning these concepts is part of the Game! It may even help to begin your mental preparation on the previous day.

Before your session, tell yourself that this is going to be a music-and-music-only day. You might want to think of it as your day to write "bad music," your day to create "audio sketches," or maybe your day to "write music really fast." Anything can work if it differentiates IMM writing, in your mind, from the songwriting process as you've come to know it all of your life.

Let's take the "bad music" idea even further: Tell yourself that you are going to *ferociously seek out* creative disaster. That's right—you read it correctly. You will strive to achieve the biggest musical and lyrical train-wrecks, the funniest bloopers, ideas that are "trite" and ideas that are "over the top," and you're going to have a great time doing it. Welcome "failure" into your life. Or, better yet, *declare war* on the whole idea of "good" and the self-imposed, socially reinforced rules that have been stifling your songwriting (see Chapter 1). You're going to be like a Viking berserker in battle, foaming at the mouth. If someone came along and chopped

CROSS THE LINE!

IN WRITING SONGS, and searching, as we do, to define and evolve the limits of the signature "sound" that sets us apart from all others, it might be said that we ultimately look for the *right balance*: tension vs. resolution, consonance vs. dissonance, beauty vs. ugliness, humor vs. seriousness. There's always a line separating any such pair of opposites, and as songwriters, we're always trying to find that line. What's the best way to find that line? *Cross it!* In your Day Session, conscientiously write a song that's much too dissonant, funny, trite, confessional, serious, etc. Remember, you can always rein something in if it will improve your song. (Later!)

off his right arm, he'd pick up the sword with his left hand and slay his enemy that way. This kind of fortitude will come in really handy when you're fighting your own battle!

Remember, writing "good" music isn't the point here. Writing a lot of music is.

If you end up writing a song that you think is "incredibly stupid," hey, guess what? That's a perfectly valid musical commentary on the process you went through that day. So what if it never makes it to your next CD? This actually brings up an important point: If you ever find yourself in an all-out songwriting emergency, locked into a gruesome uphill battle with a song that clearly has *no merit* whatsoever, you can always fall back on twisting the song in a new direction, pushing it over the edge, and turning this piece of crap into something that will make your friends laugh. You'll find that thinking about your friends laughing, and yourself laughing along with them, is a real head-clearer. (More on ways to do this in Chapter 5.)

Repeating the "Three-Minute Burn" exercise from the previous chapter is another way to help get your brain into gear for IMM writing. Actually, it can help to do any activity that is improvised, playful, and won't get you discouraged if things don't proceed in a certain way.

Do you need to get plenty of sleep the night before a session? *No!* This method isn't like other mental tasks, such as taking an exam or making an important presentation. It's about taking your brain outside of its normal, cushy comfort zone. So it's a rare case in which mental fatigue can actually help you. *A lot!* That's why a 12-hour time block is better than a four-hour block: At the end of a long block, you're punchy and loopy. You're fine with throwing caution to the wind, while your mind is doing things it ordinarily wouldn't. That's not a great idea if you're taking an exam—but when you're trying to be as creative as possible, a jelly-brained, hallucinatory mental state can be a tremendous asset. In fact, there's an ICS lodge (Bullet Lodge, Minneapolis, Minnesota) that takes advantage of this effect by encouraging its members to have marathon sessions of 16 or 18 hours or even longer.

PHYSICAL PREPARATIONS

NO, NOT STRETCHING or calisthenics (although if that gets your mental faculties going, have at it). Prepare a place where your session will happen. In the ICS we call this the "sound hole." If you're a pencil-and-manuscript-paper kind of writer, your sound hole can just be a desk and a comfortable chair. If you're a recording musician, obviously it will be your studio. Either way, isolation is key. If you have a family or roommates, make it clear that your sound hole is off limits during your sessions, except in the case of emergencies. You can't very well expect to stay in the Game if kids and dogs are constantly running through your space. You may also consider unplugging any phones in the room or taking the computer offline. You certainly don't need to stay *in* your sound hole during your entire session—a walk around the block may refresh your creative energies if you find that you're running out of gas—but try to make it difficult for distractions to come to you.

TECHNICAL PREPARATIONS

THIS APPLIES TO recording songwriters: Before your session, try to eliminate any technological obstacles that could get between yourself and creativity. For example, have a cassette recorder ready and loaded at all times, in case you come up with an idea when you don't have a mic ready to go. But, if possible, you *should* have a mic ready to go at any moment. If you have only one mic cable and you also need it to connect a direct box for your bass, get another mic cable! Try to have both the mic and the DI connected to your mixer for the whole session. Whatever instrument or instruments you play, see if you can find a way to have everything connected and ready to go for the entire session. Immersion Music Method is so much better when you can put down a bass and pick up a guitar—just like that—without having to mute, unplug, flip mixer switches, re-plug, unmute, etc.

By the way, if you find that during a session you have no patience to mute a channel before plugging or unplugging—that your moment's inspiration is more important than a loud *crack* or *pop* in your speakers—that's a good sign. The Game is working for you!

DAY SESSION TIPS

Self-discipline. At any point in your Day Session, you may find yourself back-sliding into your conventional songwriter mindset. It's very easy to do: You might come up with two or three "good" ideas, causing you to get all excited—you start thinking, Hey, this is working out great!—and suddenly the next one isn't "up to snuff." Or, you come up with an idea that's so "good," you resist letting the song go in a direction that might "ruin" it. So, you start being a conventional songwriter again, trying to make the song as "good" as it can be.

Part of the IMM process involves being aware of warning signs that you're losing your edge, and reacting in order to keep your head in the Game. Some of these warning signs are:

1. You've spent an hour on a song and it isn't close to finished.

2. You play something you've written and you think, "It's [insert negative adjective here]."

MAKE A RECORDING TEMPLATE FILE

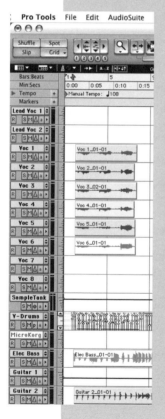

IF YOU RECORD your songs on a computer, you're used to creating a new file, adding tracks, assigning busses, etc., when you begin a new song. But when you're trying to record a bunch of songs in a day, it's not happening to have to repeat these steps each time you start a song. So, before you begin a Day Session, set up a template file that will make it as easy as possible to keep going, with few mindless interruptions. In addition to having tracks and assignments for whatever MIDI instruments you normally use, you should also have audio tracks for your usual audio instruments (bass, guitar, etc.). And you should have *a lot* of vocal tracks. Like, ten or more. Two of these should be for lead vocals, panned to center and turned up, and the rest should be for background or harmony vocals, turned down a bit and panned around the stereo field. You probably won't always use all of them—but if you need them, they'll be there. When you get a flash idea to do that 12-track Gregorian chant, do you really want your Day Session to be interrupted just so you can add more tracks? If you include in your template a pre-arranged place for just about any sound or instrument that you might record, this will never be a problem.

3. You play something you've written and you think, "It's [insert *positive ≀*

4. You scratch out a lyric.

5. You do a second take, and you play or sing exactly the same thing tha

   the first time.

6. You listen to a playback two or more times in a row without adding anything.

7. You feel tempted to discard a song in progress and pretend it never existed.

In addition, at various times in a session you can also find yourself losing interest. You might check your e-mail, or turn on the TV to check the ball game. We understand; this song-writing method can be an intense process, and sometimes you want a break from it. That's okay—to a point. Make your breaks short and well defined; if you want to take a walk out-side, for example, make it just around the block, and tell yourself that you need to come back with a new musical idea. Look for an object as you walk, and then write a song about it. This way you can make the downtime a part of the process, too.

Having fun. Even though you want your Day Session to take you outside of your comfort zone, overall, the process shouldn't be uncomfortable. Give yourself a break in non-musical areas. For now, let bad habits resume—you can deal with them later.[1] This is no day to be dieting. If eating an entire box of Cap'n Crunch will keep you happy and productive, by all means rip that thing open and let it keep you company while you write. But if a bad habit is going to hinder you, such as heavy drinking or drug use, be careful: There is a fine line be-tween creative abandon and self-destruction. Okay?

On your session day, your home should be like a nest. Beforehand, stock up the kitchen with your favorite treats. Think in advance of every kind of food or beverage that you might sudden-ly need at some point during your session, and have it ready. If you like to cook, do it the day before your session. The idea is to use your guilty pleasures and indulgences to *lure* you into the creative process. It works!

---

1. This isn't as crazy as it sounds. An IMM session isn't the kind of thing a person usually does more than two times a month. Unless your doctor tells you otherwise, it's okay to binge out on Hostess cupcakes one or two days a month, right?

Some people like to have visuals going on while they write. If you find Bruce Lee films or anime videos inspiring or energizing, by all means put one on—but turn down the sound. Most sonic distractions will work against you.

THE BURNOUT FACTOR

INVARIABLY, AT SOME point in your Day Session, you will start to feel *burnt out*. Who can blame you—you've been writing music feverishly for six or eight hours straight. You just don't

MIXING & MASTERING

IF YOU'RE A recording songwriter, the mixing process is a part of your Day Session. You're trying to come up with new songs, not the recorded tracks for songs that will be mixed on some other day. Right? So, you need to have all of your songs mixed down before the end of your Day Session. It's also important, if you will be playing your songs at a lodge meeting (see Chapter 4), that you not *remix* your songs for the meeting after your Day Session is over. In the context of a lodge meeting, that wouldn't be "fair"—presumably, the other songwriters at the meeting mixed their songs in the heat of their Day Sessions, without the benefit of a night's sleep and fresh ears. So you should, too!

When you finish your first song of the day, you'll have to decide whether to mix the song at that point, or move on and mix all of the songs at the end of your session. We recommend mixing as soon as you finish the song. It's nice to get a song "in the can" right away, and it keeps you moving forward to know that you won't have to go back and work on your earlier songs. It's a drag when you make it all the way to 20, and then you realize you're still not finished! Plus, mixing one song at a time may simply be faster, as your gear is still set up for the song you just did, and the parts are still fresh in your mind. Get the song out of the way and move on!

feel like going on any longer; you've done enough. Right? Wrong! The rules of the 20-Song Game say you're supposed to write music for 12 hours, not six or eight, or whenever you feel like stopping. There's a good reason: When you start to run out of energy, that's actually a sign that the best is yet to come. As we've noted, your brain can come up with some really interesting musical and lyrical ideas when it's tapped out, when your mental endurance is pushed to its limits. A big part of playing the 20-Song Game is actually seeing it through to its conclusion. So, don't give up! If you need a break, take a brisk walk outside, and then get back to work. When you come up with that unbelievably great song in the 11th hour of your session, you'll be glad you did.

Some people also like to give their songs a quick mastering job before they burn them to CD. Mastering is the process of performing final equalization and level tweaks to a song's stereo mix, and also of applying compression and/or limiting in order to bring up the recording's overall levels. The problems with mastering during your Day Session: (1) It's an extra time-consuming step that isn't absolutely necessary—it's time that you could use to write a new song or two, and (2) after a long recording session, your ears—and brain—are in no condition to make good decisions about EQ. For this reason, in the ICS, we allow members to remaster (but not remix!) songs before lodge meetings. But if you do decide to master your songs during your Day Session (for instance, if your meeting is that evening), try to go easy on the highs. When your ears are fatigued after 12 hours of wearing headphones or blasting the speakers, you may want to crank up that top end until the songs sound good to you. Our advice: EQ the music to sound "good," and then try pulling back on the highs to where the music is a little less bright than you'd like. When you listen to your songs the next day, you may be glad you did—and if not, you can always remaster them.

WHEN IS A SONG "DONE"?

THIS IS A QUESTION that can vex every songwriter, but especially IMM songwriters. When we're in the middle of a Day Session and the clock is ticking down, even if everything is humming along and we're having a great time, there's only so much we can do with each song. So, how do we know when it's time to move on? How much attention should be given to something before it can be considered "a song"?

This book isn't here to answer that question. IMM tells us that *anything*—even a one-second burst of white noise—can qualify as a song. Technically, if you recorded yourself saying "Boo!" at 20 different pitches, you'd be playing the 20-Song Game the way it was meant to be played. It just wouldn't be a very productive session. Yet, at the same time, spending four hours trying to get your first song "right" can really mess with your brain and throw off your session.

The decision of how far to go with any given song is a matter of balance, common sense, and your personal taste. Think of an artist making a sketch: Yes, he could draw one line and call it a day. And yes, he could whip out the gesso and oil paints and create a masterpiece. But chances are, he'll do something in between. His goal is probably to create *something* that perhaps can be developed into a full work someday—and that's our goal as IMM songwriters, too.

Most Day Sessions result in a broad mixture of songs, from undeveloped and unfinished ones to more complete ones. When you're in the middle of a song and you're on a roll, with new parts coming to you effortlessly and inspiring all sorts of exciting changes and additions, naturally you'll want to keep going. In that case, try to get enough done that you don't short-change the inspiration of the moment, but not so much that you begin to focus on detail, at the expense of other new songs you could be creating. Then there are times when you simply need to leave a song for dead. That's okay! It happens! Even if all you came up with was a pedestrian drum beat and bass line, you did create *something*—something that didn't exist before. Having done that, if need be, you can move on to the next song.

That's what playing the Game is all about: moving on. Because the next song you come up with may end up being the best you've written in your life.

THREE WAYS TO ROLL OVER PROCRASTINATION LIKE AN ARMORED TANK

A MAJOR PART of creative block has nothing to do with "inspiration"—it's the procrastination aspect. You might actually *know* what you need to do, how to fix your problem, and exactly how to do it—but you simply *can't make yourself do it*. You might read this book and like the idea of a "shotgun" approach to songwriting. But you just can't seem to get it together, schedule a Day Session, and jump in.

This can also be the central irony about "inspiration" books that tell you how to solve creative block. You read them, and they get you really pumped up. You say, "Wow! I sure am inspired!" Then a moment later, you say, "I'm hungry. What's for lunch?" Then, that turns into lunch and a matinee. A week later, the book has become an improvised mousepad. A month later, it's in the recycling bin. What happened?

To put it another way, getting yourself to implement a procrastination-solving method can be a bit like trying to find your glasses so that you can find your book—you know, the one that teaches you how to find your glasses.

If you have trouble getting started, here are three methods to rev yourself up for a Day Session:

Plan A: Form a songwriter lodge (see Chapter 4)**.** When you are all by yourself, and your schedule is a matter of whim, it's easy to drift off and become mentally isolated. What's to stop you from procrastinating? It can be hard to find leverage to pull yourself out of a rut when your entire life is happening in your head. That is why it sometimes helps to have friends. It was with this in mind that the ICS founders chose to organize their society as a ring of song-writer "lodges."

Being a member of a lodge is helpful on a number of levels, but one thing a lodge does is to serve as a kind of "procrastinator's anonymous" for songwriters who think too much. Note: In principle, a lodge can contain as few as two people, so if you know only one other musician, you are good to go!

Plan B: Schedule a "Day Pact" with a non-musician friend. The basic "buddy system" principle behind a lodge will still work, even with non-musician friends, as long as there are *buddies*. Just because your friends aren't musicians, that doesn't mean they aren't *procrastinators*. Everyone has dreams, and whatever that dream is, it is maddening when it simply won't happen. So, if you have a friend who also has a procrastination problem, chances are that they will *leap* at a chance to team up and attack it together.

Try this: Call a friend, and ask them if there is something that they've always dreamed of doing, or if there is an important chore that really needs to get done, but for some reason, they never get around to doing it. Let's say the friend says, "Yes"—it might turn out that the friend has been longing to spend a day painting, or creating a website, or cooking, or doing their taxes, or fixing up a car. Tell your friend, "I want to propose a trade. Let's set up a date in the future and institute the buddy system. We'll both get that day off. On that day, we'll both wake up, good and early, and one of us will call the other one. Then, we'll coordinate. We'll stay split up, but we'll check up on each other by phone or e-mail. I will *make sure* that you spend your day [doing what you are trying to do], and you will *make sure* that I actually do my IMM Day Session. After a nice, long day of getting things done, we'll meet somewhere, and have a little show and tell. Then, we'll go out to dinner, or rent movies, or go to a show."

A little peer pressure, a *real* deadline, and something fun to look forward to later, can be a powerful combination. (See Chapter 5 for more on Day Pacts.)

Plan C: Enroll in a class, and use the deadlines. Okay, so you don't have any friends. Fine! We can work with that! Try this: Enroll in a songwriting or recording class—whichever you prefer. Then, whenever there is an assignment, use it as a sneaky excuse to explore IMM. Then you can use your class as test bunnies, watching in glee as they try to figure out how you came up this stuff!

Important note: If you find yourself making friends in your class, and they are curious as to how you are making this music, you are in an *excellent* position to start a temporary "academic lodge." (Back to "Plan A"!)

When you boil down the idea of an academic lodge, we're basically talking about a musical "Animal House" kind of situation, where students from a conservatory or a recording school throw IMM game parties on the weekends, yell and scream, and explore less, um … "formal" modes of creativity. This is a great way to inject maverick spirit and original thinking into a scholastic setting. (An academic lodge is different from a "normal" lodge in setting only; they are run in exactly the same way. See Chapter 4 for more on lodges.)

CHAPTER FOUR

The Songwriter Lodge

"We are here to help each other get through this thing, whatever it is."

—Mark Vonnegut (Kurt's son)

A SONGWRITER LODGE is a local IMM game community—a group of musician friends who have started a weekend songwriting club, scheduling regular game sessions, supporting and encouraging each other, and meeting regularly for "listening parties," where they meet and share their work.

A typical day for a lodge starts with the members waking up, individually, in their different homes, and jumping directly into a session of the 20-Song Game.[1] Yes, that's right—the lodge members spend most of the day *split up*. The lodge meeting follows in the evening. Everyone finishes up their session, hops into their car or on their bike, and after dropping by the store to pick up snacks and beverages, they converge on a common location. They throw all of their cassettes or CDs into a pile on a

---

1. Unless the lodge is playing a special game or having a revision meeting (see Chapters 5 and 6).

table,[2] and everyone finds a comfortable chair. For the rest of the night, the lodge members take turns sharing the music they've been making all day, and regaling each other with tales from the trenches of extreme songwriting.

When you are a lodge member and you wake up on a session day, you get that extra kick in the pants of knowing that there is a guaranteed audience for every lick of music you write today. The feeling is similar to the one you get when you wake up knowing that tonight, you are going to play a show in front of a live crowd. This adds an entire new level of urgency and excitement to an IMM game session.

It's certainly possible to use the methods in this book entirely on your own. But it greatly helps to belong to a group that can support you as you work to unlearn the debilitating disease of the conventional songwriter mindset. Best of all, being part of a lodge is fun!

WHY BELONG TO A LODGE?

THERE ARE SEVERAL reasons why it helps to form a lodge or join an existing one:

Motivation. For some people, merely writing MUSIC DAY on their calendar is enough to motivate them to play the 20-Song Game. But for most folks, it's a real kick in the butt to know that there's a meeting coming up on Sunday, and that you need to bring some music to the meeting. Otherwise, you'll be teased and punched in the arm by the other members of the lodge. They put their ass on the line making music—what's your excuse? And if you do make a truckload of music that week, you can tease and arm-punch the lodge members who *didn't* put out. It's a collective way for everyone to keep each other on their toes, and push each other to work harder and get more done. All of those things are good!

"Lodge pressure." Rock & roll history has tons of examples of bands where two or more songwriters get together and push each other further and further as songwriters, locked into a creative companionship so intense that, really, the rest of the world ceases to matter; all that matters is impressing the other guy. Lennon and McCartney would probably be the

---

2. That is, if it's a home-recording lodge. For pencil-and-paper lodges, it would be a big pile of sheet music in the middle of the table. For a Nashville-style lodge, there might be no pile at all.

LODGE COMPILATIONS

AFTER A FEW meetings, make a "best of" compilation CD of the lodge members' creations, and distribute copies to the lodge. Each member's share of the music on the CD should reflect their total musical output over those sessions, not the relative "quality" of the music. In some lodges, the lodge head chooses the songs for the comp; in others, members choose their own songs, based on the feedback they received at the meetings (and maybe some of their own opinion, too). Choosing the running order and spacing of the songs is a fun project; sometimes the lodge heads do this, and sometimes members take turns putting the comps together.

ultimate example of this phenomenon. When you form a songwriter lodge, you step into a creative situation with a similar dynamic.

Knowing that you have a captive audience waiting injects a subconscious element of competition into your session: a desire to impress those guys! Naturally, this *clashes* with the volume-focused Game rules. The minute you start focusing on details, trying to make stuff more "impressive," the less volume you become capable of, and suddenly, you are in danger of "losing" the 20-Song Game![3] You do not want that to happen! This creates a kind of paradoxical tension, a crackling intensity, that we call "lodge pressure."

Every lodger deals with this pressure differently, but there is one constant: Every lodger naturally wants to do good, and see everyone smiling at the meeting when their CD is playing. But they know, above all, that the *most* embarrassing thing that could happen would be to show up at the lodge meeting with a CD containing *one half* of a song. Then they'd get arm-punched for sure!

---

3. While the 20-Song Game isn't really a game with winners and losers, it does sort of feel like you have lost when you drag your sorry butt to the meeting with one song to show for your entire session.

The human mind can do amazing things when it is under that kind of pressure. As we mentioned previously, in the Immersion Composition Society, members have at times suddenly evolved in their songwriting, production, lyric writing, everything—their abilities seeming to double from session to session, in quantum growth spurts that can span several sessions.

Having read all of that, though, when you find yourself tempted to slow down and fret about quality during a session, fight that urge! This is about producing a lot of raw material. The 20-Song Game is about radically expanding your boundaries, not making a polished album cut. And never forget: There are *a lot* of ways to impress your lodgemates, and make them smile and laugh, besides writing an obsessively tweaked, typically "impressive" song. You can impress people with the sheer number of songs you came up with, the number of minutes of music you came up with, the diversity of ideas you created, your creativity, your ability to outline and execute a big "concept" (like a 15-minute musical) in 12 hours, or the humor, fearlessness, or sheer wacked-outedness of your creations. Impress your lodgemates by staying true to the spirit of what brings you all together.

When your lodge friends are waiting at the end of the day, it is almost like you have been given a chance to perform an act of pure, abstract creation in front of a live audience—the way a good guitarist might play a brilliant, far-out guitar solo off the top of his head. It is a performance of your hidden process as a songwriter, a chance to demonstrate the full range of what you are capable of, when all of the normal rules and conventions are removed. It is an opportunity to *show them* something, to connect on a deeper level, beyond "quality." It is an opportunity to say, "This is the real me! This is *my* world." In other words, in IMM, the practice of *showing off* expands into new and exciting territories, where the possibilities become truly endless.

For all the reasons above, people who have been through the process tend to be more impressed by, say, ten short and diverse ideas than by two or three more developed, polished songs.

Support. When you boil down the idea of being an artist to its essence, you get something like this: An artist is a person who wants to do and say *new things*. Maybe this is why artists—songwriters included—are so famous for railing against conformity, bucking social conventions, and giving the impression that they don't care what anyone thinks about them.

"A true artist doesn't make art to please other people."

"If someone likes my stuff, that is incidental."

"I'm in it for the art, and that's it."

But how many artists do you know who are really like that? Have you ever noticed the way an artist friend will sometimes say that they don't care what anyone thinks about this painting, or this book that they are working on—and then, almost in the next breath, they'll say, "So, what do you think?"

Let's face it: We *care*. We pour our very essence into a creation, and if somebody doesn't like it, it's as if they don't like *us*. In a world like this, we can use some support from time to time!

The problem is, when you are frustrated creatively, it can seem like nobody you talk to knows how to give you the kind of support that you need.

When you talk to non-artists, they don't seem to understand the pressures that you, as an artist, live with every day. Underneath all of their well-intentioned words, they seem to be

SECRET SOCIETIES

AFTER A MEETING or two, with everyone intimately sharing their naked IMM creations, a lodge can quickly start to feel like a secret cloak-and-dagger society. In the Immersion Composition Society, we started inventing fantastical titles, insignias, and mottoes like some ancient fraternal order—that's where the term "lodge" came from. For example, the ICS Wig Lodge is officially *Sodalitas Mystica de Capillamento Splendido*, Latin for "the Mystical Knighthood of the Resplendent Wig." It's all in fun, but it underscores the deeper meaning behind the lodge as a place of total safety and privacy. Attending a meeting can be a powerful experience—so don't be surprised if you want to begin the next one by drawing the curtains and leading a hushed incantation.

saying, "Well, why don't you just be *normal*?" But sometimes, going to a fellow artist can be just as unhelpful—especially if that artist turns out to be even more frustrated than you! You might ask the wrong member of your local music scene for help, and get the feeling that underneath his or her advice, a smaller voice is saying, "Don't pay attention to all of those fascistic little rules that we artists think we have to follow. It is better to be free, like me. Follow *my* fascistic little rules instead!"

Sometimes, even well-meaning scene mates (e.g., the other guys in your band) can have their own *plans* and *expectations* for you. It's a bit like the way you might call your mom for emotional support, but she keeps going on and on about how she wants you to be a lawyer someday, thus making you feel even more conflicted than before.

This is why it can be such a relief to take a vacation from the big, mean, stupid world, and call all of your most trusted musical friends and form a songwriter lodge. A lodge is a place of trust and secrecy, isolated from the warring agendas and negativity of the world outside its walls. Your fellow lodgers are sworn to protect and encourage you—not as a member of some scene, or as a proponent of some artistic "movement," but as an individual. It is your duty to do the same for them. Every member is free to explore any musical impulse imaginable, to do whatever they want—no matter how far out, or how far *in!*—with the knowledge that when they show this thing they made to the gathered members of their lodge, they will get exactly the *support* that they need, no matter what.

That feels good.

For these reasons, a songwriter lodge is a lot more than a weekend music club, or a composer party circuit. A lodge is an *oasis* of sanity, freedom, safety, study, growth, privacy, and fun.

Feedback. A lodge meeting is the ideal place to showcase the songs you've written. Everybody listening knows what you went through to come up with these creations, so they're sympathetic. They understand your "miserable failures," because they're playing their own miserable failures for the group, too, and you're all laughing together. If you don't belong to a lodge, you wouldn't necessarily want to share all of your creations with anyone. And yet, as anyone who's played their songs at a meeting will attest, *you* are often the worst judge of your own music. You'll go to a meeting thinking that your kick-ass songs are tracks 3, 5, 8, and 13, but in fact, tracks 1, 2, 6, and 12 get the most enthusiastic response. Often, your "throwaways" are—at least to other listeners' ears—your best songs. How could you know this without playing *all* of your songs for your IMM compatriots? You couldn't. A lodge meeting is like a focus group where you learn how your wild creations resonate with your peers.

Meeting people. This doesn't need much explanation. A lodge is a social network of songwriters, so you're bound to form new, valuable relationships. But there's an intimacy level in a lodge that rarely exists in groups like these. At each meeting, members see (and hear) each other at their most vulnerable. You develop an almost instant understanding and trust. After several meetings, your lodge might be as closely knit as your family!

HOW TO START A LODGE

Starting a lodge is easy—just talk to your songwriter friends, explain the Immersion Music Method concept in detail, and ask if they'd be interested in giving it a try. Don't restrict your invitations to people who write the same kind of music that you do—songwriters from diverse styles can learn *a lot* from each other, and anything that helps members keep an open mind is definitely a good thing.

A lodge can consist of only two members, or dozens. Listening parties tend to be more enjoyable when there's more music with more diversity to be heard—but there are limits. If 12 people come to a 9 PM lodge meeting, and each brings 20 minutes' worth of material, obviously the meeting will last until the early morning. We've found that the optimum number of members at a meeting is somewhere around six or eight. But that doesn't mean your lodge can't have more members than that; after all, it's unlikely that every member will show up to every meeting (although 100 percent participation is a good goal to shoot for).

THE LODGE HEAD

Usually, where there is a lodge, there is a *lodge head*. This is the lodge's administrator—the person who schedules Day Sessions and meetings, and who ensures that meetings move along smoothly. He is the guy who announces that the meeting is now in session. He is the guy who yells "Next!" when it's time to put on the next CD or cassette. When the "first listen" is

POTENTIAL LODGE TYPES

HOME RECORDING. As of this writing, every lodge in the Immersion Composition Society has been a *home recording* lodge, with 12-hour recording sessions followed by an evening meeting where people share their music on CD or cassette. As you have probably noticed, much of this book's material defaults to the example of things that might happen in this kind of lodge. However, the idea of an IMM lodge can easily be tailored to other musical work styles.

PENCIL AND PAPER. This is a lodge of classical-format composers, who work on paper, with musical notation. On the morning of a session day, they all wake up in their separate homes, just like the members of a home recording lodge, and they start into their Game sessions. When it's time for the meeting, they all convene at one person's house and pile all of their charts in the middle of a table. Then, they have an informal recital. They can bring player friends, or they can do the playing themselves.

NASHVILLE. This lodge type follows the singer/songwriter format, popular in Nashville, of writing songs to be performed live—sung lyrics generally accompanied by guitar or piano. (Obviously, though, you can write for any portable instrument, and write *any* kind of music, not just folk and country!) The Day Session might involve writing down lyrics and chord changes on a pad of paper, and perhaps recording songs on a cassette recorder so that you can remember what you wrote. At the evening meeting, everyone sits in a circle, with their instruments, and they go around the circle, playing their songs for each other. Sometimes different people might accompany each other, or sing backup. If there is a piano in the corner, someone can also jump on that when it's their turn.

over, the lodge head announces intermission. After the intermission, if everyone seems to want to do a second listen, the lodge head is the guy who says, "Okay! Let's do it!" He's also the guy who yells "Shaddup!" when everyone is talking over someone's song.

If your lodge wants to keep things from getting too unilateral (with one guy being the big meeting boss all the time), you can rotate the position, with different people being lodge head at different times. Another approach is to have the lodge head position be temporarily bestowed upon whoever has volunteered to host the meeting at their home.

MEETING GUIDELINES & ETIQUETTE

Ensuring a level playing field. Make sure all participants know the rules of the 20-Song Game before their first session. If you are the lodge head, you can decide how strict you want to be. In some lodges, members do their sessions on the day of the meetings, but other lodges are more lenient. Most lodges enforce a rule that a 12-hour session cannot be broken down into two six-hour sessions—but occasionally exceptions can be made in the case of someone who, say, is married with children and wouldn't be able to make it otherwise. But *do* ask that members not use any pre-existing material, and *not* to re-mix their recorded songs on a later day in order to make them sound better. Only the original mixes from the Day Session are to be used! Otherwise, those who follow the rules will be at a disadvantage, or may feel that others have cheated in the Game.

To determine who goes first as the group's guinea pig, you can draw straws or just ask for volunteers. (In the ICS, if there's a newcomer to an established lodge—i.e., a "virgin"—that person traditionally goes first.) Each person can give a brief introduction about their session: how many songs they did, what their process was like, song titles, etc. It's fun when people bring printed copies of their song titles and even lyrics for the other members.

Once the music starts, be respectful to the writer. Keep conversation to a minimum. The Golden Rule applies here—behave the way you'd like others to behave when it's your turn. When a member's session is done playing, a round of applause is in order.

An important note on criticism. A lodger who has just shared their music with you will probably be eager to talk about it. (Why else do we share our music with other people?) On one hand, they probably want to know what you liked about their session. On the other hand, it's not unusual for a lodger to be punchy and silly after their long day, and to want to rip on one (or all) of their songs and make jokes about how awful they are. Writing dumb songs, train-wrecking on purpose, and laughing until milk shoots out of our nose is where a lot of the fun of IMM comes from. But never forget the essential vulnerability of every lodger's position, as they sit there, watching you listen to the most naked creations they have ever shown anyone. And never forget that there is a big difference between giving someone feedback and delivering an unwelcome criticism. In IMM, that line can be a fine one.

We share a lot more than our music at lodge meetings. We share the products of a cathartic creative process that temporarily renders us, in a very real sense, helpless. We give our

IMM DAY PACTS

WHEN YOU HAVE been involved with a lodge for a while, you might find that you've developed a new desire or an important goal, and you'd like to tap the power of IMM's socially reinforced deadlines to help achieve that goal—but the goal conflicts with some of IMM's requirements. For instance, you might want to take a day to work on a song you've been working on for years, but according to the rules, you aren't supposed to work on pre-existing material when you play the 20-Song Game. Frustrating, isn't it? Fear not, dear friend—IMM is way ahead of you! Whenever you find yourself with a need that can't be addressed through normal lodge and game channels, this is what an IMM "Day Pact" is for.

A Day Pact is sort of an informal, *mini* lodge meeting, between two or more lodgers—a way of scheduling "extracurricular" lodge activities. It is a day when two or more lodgers agree to correspond by phone or e-mail or, in many cases, actually hang out in the same house together, and pursue whatever special goals they want to. This may include refining ideas from the last Day Session, fellow lodgers a deeper glimpse into our naked creative process than we will likely show anyone else as long as we live. There is a kind of sacredness to that, and a person who is brave enough to open up and take a chance, with the aim to grow and to connect with people, never deserves to be shot down for having done so.

This is not to say that you need to tiptoe around your fellow lodgers with a big, fake smile, dispensing new-age blessings. ("And *you* are special, too, in your very own way!") You didn't form this cool secret songwriting club to act cheesy! You also don't need to behave as if everyone were so fragile that they'd shatter if you touched them. Lodges evolve rapidly and grow even more tight-knit over time; after a while, there develops a wordless understanding of each member's personal disposition, and in general, things just tend to get a lot more casual.

playing "hat" games and entering the results in a Start Pad (see Chapter 5), spending a day immersed in practicing an instrument, or even learning a new technology. For all of the same reasons that lodges are good in general, it can be very productive to call up a fellow lodge member and arrange to pair off, independent of the rest of your lodge. Schedule a day when both of you will spend 12 hours immersed in a specific music-related task. At the end of the day, if you have been spending the day split up, get together to blow off some steam and perhaps show each other the fruits of your labors. After that, do something fun to reward yourselves! Eat out, rent videos, or go to a show.

While IMM is a system of games, and those games have rules, don't forget that IMM is intended to be a system of musical freedom. IMM is a framework in which you set musical goals and find a way to leverage and motivate yourself toward that goal—you *make it happen*. So, if you ever feel held back by the rules and have a special need, call up a lodger or two and tell them about it. The chances are good that you will find a way to fit it into lodge life.

Also, every songwriter is different! Each person in a lodge prefers a different feedback style—they will let you know what it is. Some lodgers like their feedback loose and silly, and some are more serious about it. Some lodgers love to rip on their own stuff, and others don't like that at all. As a fellow lodger, make an effort to find out what kind of support each person wants, and then *give it to them*. Use common sense to determine what feedback each lodger wants and what they don't want—where that *line* is for them—and don't cross that line during a meeting.

This is what it means to belong to a lodge.

For those of you just starting out with a new lodge, here's a simple rule of thumb: When in doubt, be gentle, enthusiastic, and tactful. Unless a fellow lodger literally *asks you* for constructive criticism, it is generally advisable to avoid criticism altogether, and instead, to simply support that person, telling them what it is that you *like* about their song. Let that person seek out other kinds of advice and feedback at a more appropriate time and place. This is a good place to start; things will loosen up as they proceed.

Avoiding the "open mic" effect. After you have gone through the effort of forming a lodge and filling it with your songwriter friends, one thing you don't want to happen is for the lodge's creative "oasis" dynamic to be compromised, or for that dynamic to lose steam and drift off. For this reason, lodges tend to develop rules about two things. The first one is guests.

A lodge meeting is not an "open mic" where anyone can walk in off the street, eat your food, and demand a chance to present their music! Would you feel safe to try anything musically if you knew there might be a bunch of weird strangers at the meeting? You're better off playing it safe and not inviting any guests without asking the rest of the lodge first. Even better, discuss the matter of a guest policy at the beginning of one of your meetings; it might turn out that everyone in your lodge would welcome guests. It's up to each lodge to determine how loose or strict it wants to be.

Another thing that can drain the potency from lodge meetings is when people show up with random music presentations, ignoring the Game rules entirely:

"Oh, I didn't play the 20-Song Game. A friend and I just jammed for two hours and recorded it. Is that cool?"

"This is a live recording of my band playing a show last night."

"I didn't feel like aiming for volume, and I didn't feel like confining my session to one day. I've got the first half of a song that I worked on for eight days."

While it's definitely fun and healthy to mix things up now and then, lodge members should understand that meetings are for sharing the results of 20-Song-Game Day Sessions (except on special occasions; see Special Games, page 106). This is the glue that holds the lodge together. If a lodger wants to submit a presentation of music they made in a special game, or play the results of a "polish" game session, they should *also* bring a 20-Song-Game presentation, and play that *first*. (It might even be a good idea to save special presentations for the end of the meeting.) If you make sure everyone plays the 20-Song Game, each lodger will be on track

MEETING DO'S & DON'TS

WHEN COMMENTING ON someone's music at a lodge meeting,

do say things like:

"That's a really unexpected chord change—I love it!"

"Cool guitar riff."

"I like how your vocal delivery is so blasé there."

"I'm pissed off that you get such great drum sounds."

"I can totally tell that you just wanted to get done with this one."

Don't say things like:

"This sounds like a Cars throwaway."

"Do you not normally play guitar, or . . . ?"

"Have you ever heard of gain-staging?"

"How many more minutes does this song last?"

"You should write down your melodies before you try to sing them."

with the rest of the lodge, everyone's happy, and the non-Game music functions a bit like "bonus tracks." This will prevent the lodge from losing that magical quality of everyone moving toward the same goal. You don't want that to happen! As with guest policies, every lodge should decide how strict it wants to be about special presentations.

Food and refreshments. Never forget a major rule of lodge meetings: *Bring treats!* Before you go to the meeting, drop by the corner store and pick up some potato chips, salsa, pizza, drinks, cookies, ice cream, gummy bears, fondue, Twinkies, Apple Jacks, frozen cookie dough, or whatever strikes your fancy. When everyone gets to the meeting and piles up their CDs and cassettes, there should also be a piling area for food and drinks.

This rule was originally instituted in the ICS for a good reason: When you're doing a Day Session, sometimes you *forget to eat*. By the time you get to the meeting, you can be so hungry that you're on the verge of fainting. Lodgers need to be fed! Some lodges cook before the meeting and actually have "real" food. Veronica Lodge of Portland, Oregon, uses every meeting as a venue not only for their musical pursuits, but as an outlet for that lodge's towering culinary obsessions. (We forget, but there might be some actual chefs in that lodge.) You can do some cooking, too, if you want to!

First listen, intermission, and second listen: When all of the lodgers have finished playing their music, it is customary for everyone to have an intermission, go outside into the night air, look up at the stars, talk about how the day went, and give the smokers a chance to get their fix. Afterward, if the night is still young, there's often a *second* listen—all of the music gets another listen, or, more commonly, each lodger plays just the "hits" or "best of" from the session. But if the first listen was long and everyone is too sleepy, they just gather up their stuff, high-five each other, and go home.

NICHOLAS'S STORY, PART 3
Forming the ICS

FROM THE DAY of the "composer duel" onward (see Nicholas's Story, Chapter 1), the lives of Michael and me were completely altered. The 20-Song Game was an instant obsession, and it permeated *everything*. We were always calling and e-mailing each other, swapping song titles and arrangement ideas, and spurring each other to new heights of creative abandon. Every little thing we saw and heard all week long, as we went about our separate business, seemed to relate to songwriting or recording in some way. Every time one of us passed a vandalized road sign, overheard a strange scrap of conversation in a fast-food restaurant, or spied a piece of cryptic graffiti under a freeway overpass, we would ask ourselves, Would *that* make a good song title? Every time one of us heard a car horn, a jet airplane passing overhead, or a dog barking in the distance, we would say, "Could I build a song around *that* noise?" It became a joke between us; if one of us sneezed or coughed, he'd say, "I wrote that"—and both of us would crack up.

During sessions of the Game, there were no limits as to what constituted a subject worthy of being turned into a song, or a sentence that was okay to say out loud. Both of us were possessed by a new, feverish desire to try everything—to say *anything*. We wrote music about random stuff in our rooms: lamps, dirty socks, chairs, windows, coffee cups, carpets. We wrote music about things we saw when we walked around the block during a break between songs: dogs, fences, clouds, trees, cars. When we ran out of ideas, we sang about our lack of ideas. We pressed RECORD on the 4-track and sang random sentences out of books, or used the instructions on the back of a box of matches as lyrics. We wrote songs about the most *out there* subjects we could think of. We also wrote songs about the most heartfelt and relevant subjects imaginable: dreams, fears, memories, desires. At other times, we opened ourselves completely and became children again, revisiting our first innocent impressions of some movie or TV show we saw when we were nine years old.

Of course, this made us realize that the 20-Song Game constituted not only a radical approach to songwriting, but also a kind of primal, cathartic therapy. We weren't just writing music; we were *getting stuff out*. We were expressing things that we had been holding inside for our entire lives—things we had never trusted another person to understand.

Which reminds me . . . .

Like so many artists who had come before us, throughout our lives we had experienced our share of bumps, scrapes, and disappointments. In particular, we had always gotten a lot of flak from the rest of the human race for the way we walked around saying and doing unexpected stuff all the time. This should hardly surprise most readers; cruising for trouble and being deeply misunderstood is, after all, a large part of what being an artist is all about! So, after decades of grappling with relentless opposition and resistance from every side, you might say Michael and I had lost much of our faith in the human race. Have you ever felt like that—like you are surrounded by jerks all the time, and these jerks don't understand you? It's enough to make anyone want to pack up their things, walk off down some lonely interstate highway, and wander the earth like Bill Bixby in *The Incredible Hulk*.

But this is a weird way to feel when you are a songwriter. Songwriters write songs so that *people* will listen to them, right? We set out to communicate with those people! But what happens when a songwriter gets to a point in their life where they believe that nobody understands them—not really? How are you supposed to be a songwriter under those conditions?

The thing is, over the course of our lives, Michael and I had developed a deep fear of *listeners*. When we were writing music, our psychology had been that of a fugitive from justice, or an illegal alien, expecting at any moment to be *exposed* as an impostor, a fraud, a criminal, and run out of town.

When a songwriter comes to perceive the act of songwriting as something *dangerous*—something that might get us into really bad trouble—you might say that developing creative block, and finding little ways to hold ourselves back creatively, is just good common sense.

But after discovering the 20-Song Game, Michael and I didn't feel that way anymore. When we entered into this pact, we had silently agreed to *become* that trustworthy "listener" to each other. Our agreement had created a sort of halfway house for our material, a *safe* place where we could test out our fledgling material on an interested, sympathetic audience, only then deciding if we felt like polishing this song and releasing it to the public. This meant that no day of songwriting would go unrewarded ever again. It changed *everything*.

Every time we played the 20-Song Game, all of the mental noise and resistance that we had felt throughout our lives simply went away. We didn't think about mean jerks who might not like our music. For the moment, those people were removed from the equation. This wasn't *real* music—not yet! It was play-and-

Michael Mellender

research music. Nothing was off limits. Everything was encouraged. Discovering the Game was sort of like discovering a magical playroom where we could turn off gravity and float around, bouncing off the walls—a private world that we could always escape to.

Isn't that how it's supposed to be?

For all of those reasons, a lot of the music that we made in these new sessions sounded noticeably different from any music we had ever made before, in a *good* way. These songs were unconsidered, unapologetic, written with no fear of the listener whatsoever. In fact, many of these songs seemed to generously extend themselves to the listener, as if that listener were the most trusted of friends. On the other hand, there were also songs that clawed their way out of the speakers and loomed over the listener, as if it were the listener, not the artist, who should be worried! These songs made no attempt to qualify, announce, or explain themselves; they just *were*.

Maybe this is why the songs that turned out well—the "keepers," as we call them—were *so damn good*.

AS THESE SESSIONS progressed, Michael and I kept pushing each other further and further. We were, indeed, striving for quantity—that, of course, is the goal of the 20-Song Game. But, there was also this sneaky part of each of our minds that was always squirming ceaselessly, trying to figure out a way to write stuff that would make the other guy fall over in amazement. This pressure was intense, and we both felt it! It sounds like a bad thing, but it was a *good* thing. It had an incredible effect on our writing, performance, and recording abilities.

We weren't far into our new regimen when we noticed that the sophistication of our output was increasing at a ridiculous rate. We'd repeat the discoveries of every new session the next time, with more confidence, and we'd integrate them into that session's new experiments. Every new session's output seemed to be *twice* as good as the output from the session before.

We came up with so many speed-songwriting techniques during that first summer alone! Every time Michael showed up at a meeting, he would have several new anecdotes about guerrilla arrangement tricks he had made up that day, where a number of cheap, partially broken instruments could be played together to create a new, unimaginably fascinating noise, sounding to all the world like a texture produced by a chamber orchestra. Michael was literally *inventing* new instruments—discovering ways to play a bicycle wheel as a musical instrument, make two quarters rubbed together sound like a maraca, or turn a slammed door into a percussion effect.

Meanwhile, I had learned that if I laid down one line of cello (played badly) over a MIDI arrangement of keyboard strings, it often sounded amazingly similar to a full string section. My ongoing quest to find the most annoying mouth-noise ever recorded actually taught me *a lot* about singing; it fostered a new level of confidence, while laying the foundation for a new vocal persona—one that resembled my actual speaking voice in a direct, fearless way I had never dreamed possible. I was also picking up skills on drums and clarinet, two instruments that I had only just started messing around with.

We were both discovering a lot of new uses for handheld cassette recorders and blank index cards (see Chapter 5).

There was a steep improvement curve on the technological front, as well. When I had started out these sessions, I had been using a 4-track—but somewhere in my feverish quest to get better sounds faster, I had already started to record into my computer, even though I didn't have an instruction manual, or any training. I just started *doing it* one day. I had also dusted off, and was now using, every piece of music gear I could find lying around my house.

After a while, this sense of seemingly limitless progress was so intoxicating, and we were having so much fun, that we stopped meeting every other Saturday. For a period of three months or so, we started to meet *every* Saturday.

NEAR THE END of that gonzo songwriting marathon, Dave, a gypsyish guitar slinger whose singing voice sounded like the voice of Bluto in really old Popeye cartoons, started showing up at our doorstep on meeting nights, bearing CDs of his own Game music. It was at this moment that we became a society.

Thanks, Dave!

Then Morgan, a mysterious beatnik who emitted interesting squeaky monkey noises, and Mick, a wild and unhinged character who went by the stage name of Darling Freakhead, started showing up at our doorstep, too, bearing bottles of wine and bags of chips. Soon after, Matt, a cerebral multi-instrumentalist who worked on S.E.T.I. by day—and Steve, a warm and weird entomologist whose songs sounded like selections from a kiddie science-hour TV show from Mars—started showing up, too.

Now there were seven of us. Whenever one of us was burning through a Day Session, we imagined those six other faces waiting at the end of the day. We wanted to see those guys laugh, wanted to see those faces light up with

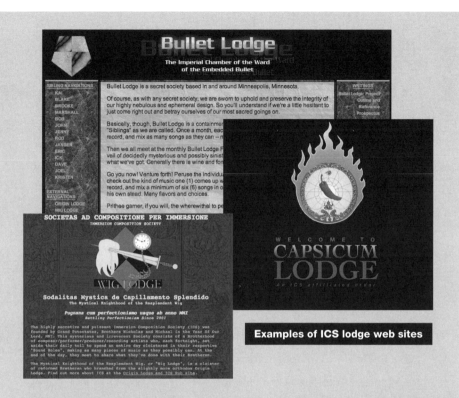

Examples of ICS lodge web sites

surprise. We were privy to each other's secret processes as songwriters. We learned from each other. We ripped each other off. We encouraged each other to be fearless—to try everything, and to say anything.

We started calling ourselves the "Immersion Composition Society."

About six months into the ICS experiment, a visiting composer, Steven Clark, asked if he could create his own splinter group. Michael and I were ecstatic, of course, and said, "Yes, please!" Thus was the mighty "Wig Lodge" born. We decided to name our local chapter "Origin Lodge."

Within a year, there were six songwriter lodges spread out between Oakland, California, and Vancouver, Canada, and the Society was growing. Michael and I were receiving e-mails from newly formed lodges all the time.

It seemed there were talented basket-cases and unmotivated visionaries *everywhere!* One by one, they were coming out of the woodwork and joining the party. Isolated dreamers whose minds burned too brightly. Passionate idealists who experienced their own titanic potential not as a source of excitement, but as a crushing weight. These were the very people who should have been building the future, because they dreamed and hoped so desperately, sitting in some basement or attic somewhere, unable to act, unable to get started—because they cared *too much*—while far less idealistic minds continued to shape the music world.

But, *these* particular dreamers and basket-cases had decided never to be silent again. They were playing games, cutting loose, and being prolific. They were ignoring the voices all around them that said, "You can't do that!" They were banding together and helping each other along.

That is why the Immersion Composition Society was formed.

That is what this book is about.

CHAPTER FIVE

The Compendium

A COLLECTION OF TECHNIQUES, TRICKS, AND GAMES FOR THE IMM SONGWRITER

"In every job that must be done,
there is an element of fun.
You find the fun, and *snap!*
The job's a game."

—Mary Poppins, "A Spoonful of Sugar"

THE FIRST FOUR chapters of this book explained how Immersion Music Method works: how to play the 20-Song Game, how to have a Day Session, and why you should belong to a lodge. This "Compendium" chapter is a grab bag of specific IMM *techniques* for you to use when you're songwriting. The Compendium consists of three sections. This first section is meant to help you play the 20-Song Game in order to generate raw material. Here, you'll find "starts"—ideas to help you begin a song from nothing—and "stucks," which are things to do when you don't know what to do next. The next two sections offer alternative themes for Day Sessions, and special games that you or an entire lodge can play.

GENERATING RAW MATERIAL

PRE-ARRANGING YOUR "STARTS"

The rules of the 20-Song Game (see page 19) specify that you bring none of your own pre-existing material to your Day Session. When we say "material," we mean actual *notes*—the rhythms and pitches—as well as the lyrics. But that doesn't mean you can't come up with some conceptual starts: genre or arrangement ideas, themes, moods, or even song titles, beforehand. During the week before your Day Session, write down some ideas for song "starts," or random phrases that you've heard—anything that can form the nucleus of a song. When you're in the midst of your session and it's time to start another song, you'll appreciate having these ideas handy so you don't have to dream one up out of a vacuum.

Alternate idea: If you're in a

Generating Raw Material

THREE ESSENTIAL TOOLS

YOU CAN MAKE your IMM sessions a lot smoother and easier by incorporating three concrete songwriting tools: the Start Pad, the Start Deck, and the Stuck Deck.

The Start Pad. Ideas for songs can come at any time of day—or night—and you won't always have a recorder handy. So, try to carry a little notepad with you at all times. If you hear an interesting spoken phrase that might form the nucleus of a song, or you have an idea for a novel sound or a unique arrangement concept, you'll always be able to write it down and use it later. When you're in the midst of a Day Session and you need some fresh ideas, it's great to be able to turn to a pad that you've scribbling in for the past month.

The Start Deck. A Start Deck is a stack of index cards that you create over time, filling it with songwriting ideas that you have picked up here and there. When you find yourself without any ideas at the beginning of the song-writing process, and you don't know where to start, you can shuffle that deck, and draw a card, any card! Then, you use the idea written on that card to kick-start your brain into action. For example:

"Write something in 5/8"

"Start on electric banjo"

"1930s film score"

"Invert instrumental roles—flute plays low, bassoon plays high"

"Forced First Take" (see page 72).

You build your Start Deck much in the same way that you keep a Start Pad. Whenever you have a good song-writing idea and go, "Hey, that's a good Start Deck idea!" you grab a blank index card, write down the idea, and add that card to your Start Deck.

You might even *transfer* particularly successful strategies from your Start Pad to your Start Deck—say, when one of your Pad ideas worked out really well for you in a session. This way, that successful songwriting tactic becomes a permanent part of your repertoire.

Keep in mind, though, that while the ideas that you write down in a Start Pad need to be used only once (e.g., in your next Day Session), the ideas that you write down in your Start Deck are designed to be shuffled and reused, again and again. For instance, when you come up with a song title, that is something you would probably use *just once*—so that would be an idea for your Start Pad, not your Start Deck.

songwriter lodge, pre-arrange with one or more of your lodgemates to come up with a set of these starts, and at the beginning of your Day Session, have a "start exchange"—each of you can work using a lodge-mate's starts, or all of you can work from the same starts. At your lodge meeting, it's great fun to hear what you all came up with independently.

STARTING SONGS

For a frustrated songwriter, nothing is more intimidating than being faced with a blank page of manuscript paper, an empty recording file, or a virgin, unblemished page from a notebook of potential lyrics. The potential for something great to happen is certainly there—but there's also the potential for ego-crushing disaster. It's at this critical moment that songwriters attempt to conjure the muse, to summon forth inspiration out of nothingness. However, the muse doesn't always answer your call, and in that case your songwriting session may be over before it even began.

That's frustrating.

But, if you've been following along, you know that Immersion Music Method is all about saying to hell with the muse as we know her. The muse doesn't need to be coaxed and conjured; we need not be at the mercy of her whims. We can *manufacture* inspiration, through IMM.

That still doesn't answer the question: When it's time to start writing a new song, where do you start? It's hard enough to start one song—how on earth do you start *20* of them?

The key lies in the mindset you adopt. You'll probably have a rough time if you go

Your deck *might* include: genre descriptions (e.g., synth-funk, taiko drumming, garage rock, Gregorian chant), instrumentation ideas (cello and harpsichord, rock trio, Moog and stick-zither), instructions ("Play your electric guitar with a violin bow"), or *any* scrap of suggestive text that might inspire you ("still life with meteor shower," "pastoral night scene," "anime dystopia").

Obviously, you can also transfer some of this chapter's starts into your Start Deck, but it's a lot more fun, and a lot more personal, when your Deck is filled with the kinds of things that you already like to do.

The Stuck Deck. Similar to the Start Deck, the Stuck Deck gives you random ideas for how to move on when you get mired down while writing a song. As with the Start Deck, many of these ideas can be taken from this chapter, but we heartily recommend generating your own ideas as well. Tip: Grab a stack of blank index cards and put on a CD of the most creative, inspiring music in your collection, and when you hear something interesting—a dropped beat here, a switch to waltz time there, a minor-3rd modulation—write it on a card. Then, when you're songwriting and you get stuck, pull a card from the deck and *do what it says*. No matter what the card says, resolve that you will make it work artistically, and don't back down. You'll be amazed at what can happen when you "force" yourself to do something musically that you otherwise wouldn't think to do.

"HAT" GAMES

ICS LODGES SOMETIMES use "hat" games at meetings to pre-plan starts, and the most interesting thing about the custom is that it happened all over the Society without anyone discussing it. One day, we all realized we were doing it. When Bullet Lodge (Minneapolis, Minnesota) has "hat" drawings, they call it "Target Practice." Origin Lodge refers to our "hat" game, unsurprisingly, as "Hat."

It works like this: Get together with a friend, or, if you are a member of a lodge, the entire lodge during a meeting. Everyone gets a pad of paper and a pen. Then, everyone spends time writing down little song ideas or instructions, song titles, random sentences, genres, or instrumentations—and then they cut or tear them off the page, creating little scraps of paper with song ideas on them. They fold up those pieces of paper and throw them into a hat or a grocery bag, or whatever is lying around that might suit the purpose. At the end, there is a drawing. Everyone reaches into the hat and grabs a scrap of paper (or more, depending). It's a bit like cracking open your fortune cookies at a Chinese restaurant: Everyone oohs and ahs, and looks over each other's shoulders, and reads their instructional paper scraps aloud to each other, and laughs, and wants to know what this person or that person got.

It is now the option of everyone involved to incorporate the song idea(s) from the "hat" game into their next Day Session. This can be an amazingly useful way to write

into the process thinking of it as some kind of *test* that will reveal how good or bad a songwriter you are, or if you treat the situation like a school assignment, in which your work will be evaluated by some overseeing authority. Remember, you're playing a game! Getting all self-conscious and stressed out can affect your performance in *any* game— especially a creative one like the 20-Song Game.

Instead, when it's time to start a song, try to be *playful, explorational*, and *random*. Mind you, this doesn't mean your song will necessarily turn out whimsical or bizarre; as a songwriter you will naturally take it in whatever direction it needs to go. But no matter what kind of songs you tend to write or want to write, understand that it really doesn't matter where you start. A song that started out being about the chair you are sitting in, may end up exploring the meaninglessness of life. A song about the pencil in your hand may end up being about your dead-end job, and a song about the clock on the wall may end up as a feel-good party track with a chorus that goes, "Everybody say *yeahhh-uhh!*" So, when starting, try not to consider the task before you, or ponder what may or may not happen. You need not attempt to conjure or summon anything. Simply take a breath and start somewhere—anywhere. Pull a random word out of a random book on your bookshelf and start from there. Start a song by writing about your lack of ideas. In IMM, starting isn't the point; the point is to build, play, and move ahead.

Still, we thought you'd appreciate having a bunch of outside of your comfort area, and to explore radically new territories, growing as a songwriter in the process.

An entertaining variation: If you drew three pieces of paper with three separate songwriting ideas or sentences, try stapling two or more of those paper scraps together, creating *one* big, complicated set of instructions that have to be incorporated into *one* song (for example, "generate random number sequence" + "style: lounge music" + "guitars up to 11"). This can produce fascinating results—sometimes funny, sometimes beautiful—and you might even stumble on a useful new sound you (or anyone else) had never thought of before.

There are many other possible variations. In fact, there really is no end to what can be turned into a "hat" game. IMM Day Pacts (see page 50) are a great place to explore these possibilities. With a little ingenuity, two or more people can use a "hat" game to create randomized stories, poems, instructions, plots for musicals and operas to be written in one day, or even notated pitches and rhythms. The list goes on and on. Make up your own "hat" games, and invite your friends to join in!

ALL ABOUT THE NOTES

A LOT OF the greatest music ever written has one thing in common: *melodies*. In pop songwriting, this might take the form of the song's "hook," a clever, pithy melody that worms its way into the listener's brain, making that song unforgettable. In classical composition, melodic lines often take the form of a central "theme" that repeats in different ways, appearing here and there in altered or replicated forms, functioning a bit like the composition's DNA. So, while it can be equally productive and enjoyable to build music around chords and rhythms, if you're interested in broadening your horizons and attacking songwriting from every conceivable angle, don't forget to orient some of your IMM session time toward experimenting with single-note lines!

PUT ONE NOTE AFTER ANOTHER

START! When you're writing a melody, sometimes listening to the whole thing gives you too much information—it might cause you to write too predictably, or lapse into territory that feels clichéd. To breathe freshness into your melodies, try this: Pick any two notes, with any intervallic distance between them and with any durations, and start to write a melody beginning with those two notes. Let the notes' pitches and rhythms suggest more notes, until you have constructed a section of a musical phrase, a small fragment of a melody that is not finished yet. It might be three notes, four notes, or five notes. Then—and this is important—intentionally "forget" where the melody began, and continue writing the melody based only on the last couple of notes you wrote. You might repeat this process—forgetting where you started, and adding to the single-note line—several times. Don't listen to the melody as a whole until you're finished writing it! This

"recipes" for starting songs. That's exactly what the starts in this chapter are for—they're tricks for getting past the starting stage as quickly as possible, a bit like cracking open an egg to make an omelet.

ADAPTING STARTS FOR LYRICS

Most of the starts in this chapter are described to get you going on the musical part of a song. However, many of them can be adapted for writing *words* as well as notes. For example, you can use The Radio (see page 86) and spin lyrical ideas from the words on songs that you hear, or you can Put on Blinders (see page 74) while writing a lyric—doing so may take the song in a new, more interesting direction. Get creative with the starts and stucks— each of them can be used in a lot more than one way.

THE "SCRAMBLED EGGS" EFFECT

It's well known that when Paul McCartney was writing "Yesterday," the working title was "Scrambled Eggs." Now, a lot of songwriters would not let a pretty ballad about breakfast get very far—the idea is much too "stupid," "dumb," or "moronic." But that never stopped Paul. He had already hammered out the tune's music, but to prevent only being able to hum the melody, he wrote some words (probably very quickly): "Scrambled eggs / Have an omelet with some Muenster cheese / Put your dishes in the washbin please / So I can clean the scrambled eggs." After he had finished writing a working lyric, *then* he went about writing the real words, which of course would become immortal.

The lesson here? *It doesn't*

technique can result in beautifully twisting, unpredictable melodic lines that are extremely fun to harmonize over and develop.

THE FORCED FIRST TAKE

 Pick up an instrument and give yourself ten or 15 seconds to come up with a quick theme, riff, or melody. If you are technology user, record it. *Actually time yourself* with a stopwatch or digital timer—and don't go over the limit! No matter what you came up with in those few seconds, *without changing the note sequence at all*, build a song around what you wrote.

This technique can produce some wonderful, outside-the-box writing, as your mind struggles to build strong music out of a weak theme, build rhythmic music out of an arrhythmic source riff, or locate a new tone center that recontextualizes an ugly clam into a pretty polychord. After toiling away like that for a while, you might notice that when you remove the original 15-second source theme, what you are left with is a fascinating sequence of backing music, primed for whatever new melody you decide to lay down. Tip: You might start building on your source theme by writing a counterpoint line, imposing different keys, or creating a rhythmic pattern that complements it.

RUNNING NUMBERS

START! Choose a bunch of random numbers—by rolling dice, or by taking the numbers off of a receipt or some weird computer printout—and use them to compose something. For example, use the numbers to designate pitches (a 12-sided Dungeons & Dragons die is perfect for this if you can find one), and write a melody based on the pitches. Or—and this is great for coming up with wild, Zappa-like stuff—use the numbers to designate rhythms. For example, the sequence "91362477" could specify a bar of nine, followed by a bar of one, then three, etc.; or you can group the numerals, for example, a bar of nine, followed by a bar of 13, then a bar of six, etc. If you're really into it, turn a string of numbers into tuplets: "7256" becomes a septuplet, a duplet, a quintuplet, and a sextuplet. There is no correct way to do this—use your imagination!

START FROM THE MIDDLE (OR THE END)

START! Who says you have to start a song at the *beginning*? It's just as valid to start a song in the middle of a verse, or the middle of a chorus, or even at the very end. Pick an interesting chord, make that the last chord of the song (or chorus, etc.), and working backward, try to figure out a way for the song or chorus to end on that chord. Or, write a line of a lyric, and find a way to lyrically get to that line and continue on from that line, forming a complete verse. Write the end of a bridge first and work from there. Mix it up!

matter how you start writing *a song!* If your first attempt to write a lyric comes out "moronic," who cares? With IMM, you have the perfect excuse: You had to write the damn thing in three-and-a-half minutes. Just how good could the words possibly be?

And yet, for some songs, your "moronic" first attempt may fit perfectly. Or, the next day, that lyric you felt so ashamed of might actually look like one of your best. Decide *later*, when your head is clear and you have 20 new songs to sort through, which ones are worth developing, and of those, what needs to be changed or improved. You have your whole life to do this! And remember, once you write a song, no matter how "moronic" it may seem at the time, it is yours, and you may do with it whatever you like. Forever!

THE SONG'S CONCEPTION

Whether it's rhythm at the bottom or a hook at the top, or something in between, every song starts with a core idea—a nucleus of sorts. Upon this nucleus, other ideas are applied, layer by layer. All you need to do is come up with a nucleus, and you're on your way. After all, if you have an idea, whatever that idea may be, your songwriting page—whether literally or figuratively—is no longer blank. Right?

Here are a few examples of ways that songs can be conceived, starting with a "nucleus" idea:

• You want to try writing a song that alternates, bar by bar, between a 3/4 waltz feel and a straight 4/4.

• You hear a phrase spoken during an infomercial. It

TRANSPOSE SOMETHING

 Take one of the parts of your song, such as the bass line, and transpose it up or down by a fixed interval and see what happens. Keep your mind open; this technique can produce bizarre and dissonant results, but you just might stumble on a combination you otherwise never would have considered. If one interval transposition isn't working, try a different interval. You can transpose any part up or down in 11 different ways (one for each new key center), so one of them may tickle your fancy and suggest other new parts to be added. In general, this is a great way to "break out of the box"—a way to encourage yourself to try things that are outside your normal melodic or harmonic comfort zones.

SHIFT SOMETHING IN TIME

 Move a part forward or backward by an eighth-note, a quarter-note, or a half-note and see what happens. (If you're a recording songwriter working on a computer, this is really easy, so you can try all sorts of things in a short amount of time.) As with transposition, the possibilities are many, and you may stumble on something that's beautifully weird.

PUT ON BLINDERS

 Related to the start called Put One Note After Another (above), this technique requires you to "forget" what you've done in

order to breathe some freshness into a song. This can take the form of writing a part based on only one other part (such as a melody based only on a bass line and not the chord progression), or writing a chorus based only on the piano riff in the intro—or a chorus based on nothing at all. If you're recording, actually *mute* all of the tracks except one (or use the SOLO button), and play along with just the one track. It helps to clear your head first, by working on another song for a while, taking a quick walk, listening to something else for a minute, etc. The Blinders technique can result in parts that sound "wrong" or disjointed, but after a few listens, you'll be surprised how "right" they begin to sound. (You can always correct things if you choose to revise and polish the song.)

ALL ABOUT THE WORDS

DEPENDING ON THE genre of music, the words can be just as important to a song—or more important—than the musical notes that accompany them. If you are a classic singer/songwriter, an entire song can flow from a street sign you passed in the street, or the final sentence of a letter you got from someone—and really, those words can be the most important thing about that song.

On the other hand, if you are more of a composer/producer-style songwriter, lyrics can represent this agonizing final stage of song construction, where the wordless territory of melodies, rhythms, and chord colors that

makes you laugh, and you want to write a song using that phrase as the hook.

• You are curious what it would sound like if you combined bossa nova with Korean court music.

• You decide to start with acoustic guitar playing staccato chords in a quarter-note feel, with the first chord change going down by a half-step.

• You still haven't recovered from your girlfriend dumping you last year, and your feelings are perfectly expressed in a brief phrase (like "you destroyed my life," or something more colorful). You want to build a song around this phrase, and you want the note choices and the vocal delivery to reflect your feelings.

• You want to build a pop song from the first four notes of Beethoven's Fifth Symphony, but in a major key.

• You have a wind-up toy monkey that makes a cackling noise. The laughter suggests a rhythm, and you want to turn it into a song.

You get the idea. The nucleus of a song can be anything—an audible sound, an imagined sound, or just a concept. It gives your creative mind something to latch onto and build around.

TWO STARTING APPROACHES: "RHYTHM UP" VS. "HOOK DOWN"

Although there are many ways to start writing a song, most of them fall into one of two categories: starting from the bottom, or starting from the top. In the first approach, "rhythm up," you begin with a rhythm-section part: a drum beat, metrical idea, bass line, or chord progression. Like a building's foundation, the basic framework of the song is

you are native to suddenly has to have *words* imposed on it, so that you'll have something to *sing* over this thing.

When you are in the midst of playing the 20-Song Game, you write a lot of stuff that isn't exactly finished. The lyric to a song might end up containing a couple of really potent lines, and then a bunch of babbling noises, or even lines that contain a sort of tossed-off jokiness—but again, the idea is to get started so that you can develop this thing more later, so it doesn't exactly matter how much of the words are completely done, right?

This fact means that, in a very real way, you are free to use anything—even total garbage—as the lyric for an IMM song. But on the other hand, it also frees you up to say things that are very honest, candid, and observational. You can say pretty much whatever you want. Isn't it grand? When you are playing the 20-Song Game, never forget that you have this freedom! You don't have to grind and fester on a line, trying to get it perfect.

In fact, if you are the kind of songwriter who prefers to think of your voice as just another pitched instrument in a musical arrangement, and you are just looking for something—anything—to sing, check out the section called Using Existing Text (page 82). It provides numerous ways that an IMM songwriter can incorporate randomization and "placeholder" text into their lyrics. But first things first! This section right here contains helpful recipes for rapidly finding some words that mean something to you, and developing those words into lyrics during an IMM Day Session.

LOOK AT A PICTURE

START! A lot of great songs use rich descriptions to "paint" a picture with words. So, find an interesting photograph or painting, and start writing a lyric based on what you see. Art history books, photography books, and *National Geographic* are all excellent sources. Your words do not need to be literal and representational; you can create a story inspired by what you see. If you do describe the picture, try "painting" an impressionistic description by touching only on certain elements. A great example of this lyric-writing style is Pearl Jam's "Daughter," which begins, "Alone ... listless ... breakfast table in an otherwise empty room ... young girl ... violins . . . ."

LYRIC FREEWRITING

START! Pick a concept that you'd like to try writing a song on. For example, recently you may have experienced an emotional state that was unfamiliar to you, so you want to try writing a song about unfamiliar emotions. Get out a clean sheet of paper (or create a blank text file on the computer), and just start writing words, phrases, and sentences about that concept. Let your mind run free, and write down whatever pops into your head. Every so often, look back at what you've written for an interesting phrase or line and see if any musical ideas come to you. Sometimes if you've written a line that suggests a certain meter or stress pattern, the meter

laid down, and then other elements are applied to this framework. Most songs in hip-hop, dance, electronica, etc., were started this way. In the "hook down" approach, the song begins with a melodic or lyrical idea, or a riff, which often ends up as part of the chorus. You know, something catchy! Think of the chorus of "Who Let the Dogs Out" (can you actually remember anything *except* the chorus?) or Led Zeppelin's "Heartbreaker" riff. In hook-down songwriting the catchy bit comes first, and everything else is applied to support this catchy bit.

Some people do better with one approach than the other. If you're a drummer or bass player, or you otherwise have a good sense of the groove, rhythm up may be your thing; if your specialty is coming up with riffs and vocal hooks, naturally your best songs may come from the hook-down approach. But as an IMM songwriter, don't limit yourself! After coming up with eight or ten bass-and-drums grooves, you'll probably be itching to try a different angle. It can be pretty tedious starting a dozen or more songs the exact same way—plus, it becomes a real challenge to keep them from sounding like mere variations on one song. As we've mentioned, using an "assembly line" method can help you get through more songs faster—but a diversity of sounds, styles, and approaches are all good things when you're playing the 20-Song Game.

SHAKE THINGS UP

When you're playing the 20-Song Game, try mixing up your pattern will in turn suggest a melody or some other musical direction. If something like this comes to you, grab your handheld cassette recorder (see page 87) and sing into it to capture the idea. Then keep going—write some more words and see if they suggest any other ideas.

After just a few minutes of this, you'll likely have enough little musical nuggets and lyrical ideas to get started on a song. Save that sheet of free-association lyrics—they might come in handy while you're developing your song, or even later when you're revising it.

CHAIN & COMPARE

 Choose a word—any word. Now, using that word as a starting point, write down a chain of free-associated words, each based on the one before it. For example, if the initial word is "triangle," that might suggest "pyramids," which in turn might suggest "tomb." Before long you'll have a chain of words, something like: triangle, pyramids, tomb, candles, soap, bath, water, ocean, whale, Moby Dick, Melville, Shakespeare, fairies, forest.

After you've generated a chain like this (or a longer one), pause and look over the words. See if any two words—and they don't have to be next to each other in the chain—trigger an image, mood, etc. For example, in this chain, "triangle + water" might make you think of the Bermuda Triangle. "Pyramids + forest" might bring to mind the Mayan culture, and "fairies + ocean" may suggest the Sirens, the mythological creatures that would lure sailors to their doom. So, how about a song about Sirens of the Bermuda Triangle, or Mayan Sirens of the forest? Why not? Take one of those concepts for a spin and see where the song takes you.

Variation: If you'd like to focus your lyrical attention a bit more, try to "rein in" your associations so they remain in the particular area of imagery that the first word suggested. For example, you might generate the chain: pyramid, candles, tomb, Egypt, palm trees, Anubis, Cairo, 1920s, Indiana Jones. Now you have a list of related words or phrases that all evoke a similar theme, so once you find a pair that triggers a song idea (like "Candles of Cairo"), you can incorporate more of them into your lyric.

ALLITERATION ATTACK

START! Choose a random word (perhaps by using the Dictionary method on page 83), and then come up with another word that starts with the same letter or combination of letters, or which starts with a similar sound. Try to come up with a phrase that's somehow unique, interesting, or provocative—like "Sultans of Swing." (Sorry, that one has been taken.) Then, spin a rough lyric based on that phrase, keeping in mind the imagery it suggests. There are hundreds of hit songs with alliterative titles, and there's a reason for that: Alliteration pleases the ear and draws the listener in. It's a great way to create a linguistic hook, and combined

methodology a bit. For example, if you're a guitarist who plays hard rock exclusively, keep in mind that you don't *have* to start off every song with a fat guitar riff. Even though this approach has its benefits—say, by forcing you to come up with 20 new guitar riffs—the Game will serve you even better if you use it to *shake up* your songwriter preconceptions. Have fun with the 20-Song Game; don't feel that you have to go through your usual songwriting routines, only faster.

Of course, you can have an extremely productive Day Session by starting every song with a riff. Combined with the assembly-line work style (see Chapter 2), this can result in a bunch of songs that are actually subtle variations of each other—and when it comes time to revise and polish, you'll have a lot of material to work with. However, you may find yourself falling into a creative "box," one in which you eventually feel trapped. That's why it can be good to start a few songs with the melody, a few with words, and a few with a drum beat, etc. Mix it up.

If you do want to stick to one starting method, try varying *that* approach—for example, writing riffs at an extremely broad range of tempos, or using different meters, or unusual syncopations. Go for variety. Think of Darwin's natural selection theory: The more numerous and diverse your offspring (songs), the greater the chance that some of them will be fit (good) enough to survive and produce more offspring (be developed into really good songs).

with a good musical hook, the result can be a song that's unforgettable.

"WOOLY BULLY" FOR YOU

 Find two words that rhyme and form an interesting pair, even if they aren't typically associated with each other. (A rhyming dictionary comes in handy for this.) Look for words that sound good together and evoke some kind of imagery or mood. Then, think about the pair of words, and start freewriting about what it brings to mind.

Now, the song "Wooly Bully" may not have the world's most brilliant lyric, but it *is* amusing and colorful, and there's no denying that it's a well-loved, classic song. Let's hope that your "Wooly Bully" gets as much airplay as the original!

SAY IT OUT LOUD

STUCK? Give the direct approach a chance! Sometimes, it can be a huge relief—even a mind-blower—just to allow yourself to say one of those little things that people don't normally say out loud, to say *exactly* what you think, and see where it leads you.

During a songwriting session, as you reach further and further for the most clever way to say something, sometimes you get to a little impasse where you can't remember what you meant to say in the first place. When that happens, try "saying it out loud" to bust out of that mental rut. Ask yourself: How do I feel? How do all of my body parts feel? My stomach, my elbows, my head, my shoulders? Let's say your shoulders feel tense—is there an emotion causing that? Is there a life event that caused that emotion? Bad day at the office? Romantic trouble? Next, ask yourself: Where am I sitting right now? Ah, I am sitting in a room, writing a song. What am I looking at right now? A lamp? A wall poster? A desk?

Now, beginning from this childlike, observational standpoint, start writing. Write everything you can think of, everything you know. This might produce a spark of candid insight that sort of cuts through the crap, like: "My eyes hurt, because I am tense, because I was thinking about this one day in high school when this other kid punched me in the arm in woodshop." With a little massaging, that might form the kernel of a probingly confessional song about your teenage years, eliciting a thrill of recognition in a listener, connecting on a deeper level than a merely *crafty* lyric could have.

You also might write something a bit less insightful, like, "I have to go pee." That might end up being an incredibly funny 30-second "filler" song, one that makes your friends laugh so hard at the lodge meeting that their stomach muscles ache for an entire week.

When you use this approach, you never know where you'll end up! But no matter where the song goes, you will always know that at least this once, you came out and bravely said the exact, unfiltered, unedited truth.

WHEN YOU GET STUCK

Even when you're blazing through a Day Session, occasionally there are times when your creativity seems to screech to a halt. You just have no idea what to add to the song you're working on. One solution is simple enough—move on and come back to it later. You'll often find yourself in a different state of mind when you return to the song, and a new part may come to you immediately. However, it's kind of a drag knowing that you'll eventually need to return to a song that created a roadblock for your session. So, for the sake of keeping things flowing and progressing forward, it's often preferable to "finish up" the song one way or another. The "stucks" in this chapter are there to help you keep your session moving. It also greatly helps to have a "Stuck Deck," a stack of cards with random ideas to get you back on track (see page 68).

COPYING & COPYRIGHTS

A few of the methods suggested in this chapter involve using someone else's song as a springboard for your own ideas. There's nothing wrong with that at all; as someone once said, "Good composers borrow, but great composers steal." But keep in mind the lessons of Negativland, a group that made its mark by chopping up and deconstructing famous songs by people like Michael Jackson and U2. Negativland's creations are artistically brilliant, but their methods got them into serious legal trouble. Similarly, when you start a song with someone else's song, you should consider the issue of

USING EXISTING TEXT

Everyone agrees that writing lyrics is a major part of the songwriting process—a lyric can make or break a song. However, sometimes lyric-writing can get in the way of the musical part of songwriting. At times like this, it's best to write the words *last*, after the notes, chords, and the rest are down. At the very least, IMM songwriters should not feel like musical and lyrical creation need to happen at the same time. Often, all you need is placeholder words while you concentrate on the musical aspects. (See The "Scrambled Eggs" Effect, page 72.)

Whether you're looking for some temporary words or you need something inspiring to "spin" music from, it's often useful to turn to pre-existing text during your Day Session. (As long as they aren't song lyrics that you've written in advance, using existing text is perfectly allowed by the rules of the 20-Song Game.) Doing so makes for one less thing to have to worry about during your Day Session.

RANDOM BOOK, RANDOM PAGE

START! This is a great way to generate placeholder text, when there's no time to write real lyrics, but you really want there to be singing in that spot. Grab a random book off a shelf, turn to a random page, choose a random sentence, and *wham!* Your song now has words. If you're recording this, push

RECORD and start singing! It's pretty much that simple—but if you're a technology user, try this interesting variation: Record a few takes of random book-sentence singing, and then make a quick vocal edit based on which words from which take "sang" best. This produces a kind of lyrical cut-up effect that changes the voice's role into that of just another pitched instrument. Readers who enjoy bands that employ made-up languages (e.g., the Cocteau Twins, Dead Can Dance) will no doubt enjoy the results. Remember, you can always write real lyrics later!

OLD LYRICS, NEW SONG

START! Grab a lyric sheet from a CD—it might be one of your favorites, or something you've never heard before. Then, use the words from one song as a placeholder lyric to spin a new song that's musically completely different from the original. It can be especially challenging (but fun) to start from words that are really familiar, like "Yellow Submarine." Then, when you've finished writing the music, throw out the original lyric and write new words. (If necessary, you can wait until you revise the song to rewrite the words.) You've just used someone else's lyric to "trick" yourself into writing an entirely new piece of music—how cool is that?

THE DICTIONARY

START! Open a dictionary and find a random word. Consider the word and its definition for a moment, perhaps put the word into a

copyright infringement.

If you want to be an idealist artist and be truly free in your art, go ahead—blatantly and triumphantly rip off other artists in as bold a fashion as Negativland. It can be really fun, at least in the company of just you and your friends. But understand that you may be limiting your future options with this music. If you do violate someone's copyright, you won't be able to do much commercially with your song without first getting a mechanical license from the copyright holder, or making some major revisions.

Anytime you're writing a song that started out as someone else's, it never hurts to change it enough so that it becomes unrecognizable. That way you ensure that your new song really is yours, and all of your future options remain open.

SONGWRITING IN THE "WRONG" STATE OF MIND

The IMM system of time-pressure composition is fairly unique in the way it requires you to schedule your songwriting sessions. But let's face it: There are times when you just don't feel like writing music. Perhaps you're going through a personal crisis, having problems with a relationship, and you don't feel up to writing the happy, optimistic songs that you ordinarily write. Or, maybe you just woke up feeling sick to your stomach. In such a state, you might be tempted to skip out on your Day Session altogether. Our advice: *Don't!* Resist the urge to cave in to how you're feeling; don't allow it to kill what could be a very productive day. Instead—and you may have to fight yourself to do this—think of your Day

phrase, and then sing the word and/or phrase and anything else that comes to mind with it. Don't think, just sing something—anything! Then capture it and use it as a start for one of your songs.

DRAWING FROM OTHER PEOPLE'S MUSIC

"You can't just rip off someone else's music, you know!"

Actually, yes, you can! The finest artistic minds on the planet have been ripping each other off like crazy since time immemorial. Classical composers have a long and rich history of borrowing themes from earlier pieces and writing entire works based on them. Dozens of jazz standards are based on the chord progression of one George Gershwin song, "I Got Rhythm." (Rhythm changes, as they are called, may rank as the most common chord progression in jazz after the 12-bar blues form.) Although they ran into some trouble with copyright issues, Led Zeppelin drew heavily from old blues standards for many of their early songs. The song that first popularized rap, the Sugar Hill Gang's "Rapper's Delight," is based entirely on the bass line of Chic's "Good Times," and the Fugees scored a hit with their twist on Roberta Flack's "Killing Me Softly." And for the last 20 years or so, numerous other songs that sample riffs from Old School R&B and rock bands—including Led Zeppelin!—have populated the airwaves.

Not only are there dozens of perfectly respectable

ways to *directly* utilize an existing piece of music (cover songs, sampling, parody), it can also be marvelously productive to use a small chunk of an existing piece of music as a loose compositional springboard during a Day Session, creating a new piece of music that has absolutely no resemblance to the source material. After you've inverted, truncated, extrapolated, erased, replaced, and stomped on a lifted musical phrase for a while, there comes a moment when that original phrase simply isn't there anymore, and the song you are working on ceases to have any connection to its source material. The song is all yours now.

Sometimes, the very act of *listening* to some pre-existing music during a Day Session can have a massively rejuvenating effect on the mind, delivering a much-needed energy boost—a welcome thing when you've been going for seven hours straight and your eyes are starting to cross. Popping in a CD can also have the powerful effect of reminding you what a certain style of music *sounds* like, how it is put together, and what some of that style's clichés and tendencies are (e.g., horn stabs, turnarounds, fills)—which can help you to make something new that has a similar feel.

Remember that while the rules of the 20-Song Game (see page 19) specify that you not use any of your own existing music in your Day Session, the rules do say that you can draw on the material of other songwriters and composers from music history for inspiration. This rule was added on the behalf of songwriters for whom sampling, quoting, and theme-grabbing was part of their normal

Session as a *job* that you absolutely, positively cannot call in sick for. Vow to yourself that you will use your state of mind to your advantage. If you're angry, write angry music; if you've got the flu and you're delirious, write some woozy, delirious music.

You might be amazed what happens. You may have never written an angry, brooding, or delirious song in your life, but you may well find IMM opening up unfamiliar musical channels. This can result in a really interesting Day Session—songs that are very much outside your normal songwriting world. In fact, historically, many an ICS member has written a piece of *breakthrough* material on a day when they were sick, or run down, and their brain was all screwed up in some interesting way.

Even if you never do anything serious with these songs, it's important to go through the experience and find out what comes out of it. The process can be hugely cathartic—and if nothing else, the extreme demands of the 20-Song Game may take your mind off your current state of mind, even while it's the subject matter for all of the songs you write.

SELF-REFLEXIVE SONGS

When you're playing the 20-Song Game, don't be afraid to write a song about playing the 20-Song Game! In fact, if you're doing it right, you may have a hard time *not* writing a self-reflexive song that comments on your Day Session progress. Particularly late in your session, you may find yourself writing about how drained you are feeling, or how this song

working style, so that they wouldn't have their hands tied when they played the 20-Song Game. So, the next time you're looking for a way to inject some fresh inspiration into a Day Session, grab a random CD off a random shelf, select a random track, and see where it takes you.

THE RADIO

 Turn on the radio to a music station— whether you normally listen to this type of music or not. Then, "spin" off a song, based on what you're hearing—use the radio song as a jumping-off point. This can go in many different directions: You might write something in the style of the radio song, or something that satirizes the radio song. Or, you could write a song *about* the radio song (how much do you really hate that boy band's music?). Another approach is to borrow a phrase or a small sequence of notes and spin a tune from that. Put the sequence into a musical blender on the FRAPPE setting—invert it, change the tempo drastically, or use it as a bass line instead of a melody, or vice versa. Turn it from major to minor or minor to major. Alter the meter. Drop a couple of notes, or insert a couple. If you're trying to write an original song (as opposed to a parody, or something that you actually want to sound like the radio song), be sure to make it sound totally different from the source song.

THE REVERSE

One of the most famous starts in rock & roll history involved the

Beatles' "Because," from *Abbey Road*. Yoko Ono was playing Beethoven's "Moonlight" sonata, and John wondered what would happen if he ran the chords in reverse. A few changes and lyric additions later, one of the group's most beautiful songs was written.

There are several ways to start a song by reversing something already in existence. In addition to reversing the chords, you can begin by reversing a melody and seeing what the reversed sequence of notes musically suggests.

THE MELODY ANAGRAM

START! Pick a melody of somebody's song, figure out the notes and rhythms, and then create an anagram of the melody by rearranging the notes, giving each note the same duration that it had in the original. You can rearrange the notes in a deliberate way, or you can mix them up at random. In either case, avoid creating a "sound-alike" version of the song; in accordance with the 20-Song Game rules, make sure that you create something original—something that sounds nothing like the source song.

THE HANDHELD CASSETTE RECORDER

For those of us with home recording studios, as we expand and upgrade our gear

isn't worthy of lyrics, or how it's time to move on to the next song. This is all part of the Game! Of course, you can always change the words later, if you decide one of these songs is good enough to turn into a "real" song. Until then, write about whatever is on your mind—almost inevitably, the intensive process of IMM will be a major theme.

over the years, a funny thing happens: Our recording tools become increasingly powerful, but at the same time, they become increasingly cumbersome. Perhaps in your early days, if you had an idea for a song, you plugged a mic straight into a cassette 4-track and were good to go. But these days, maybe you have to *turn on your computer*, switch on some outboard gear, turn on the phantom power, etc., etc., before you can record a single note. Even if you're in the middle of your Day Session and you've got everything turned on and set up, if you get an idea for a song while you're in the middle of another one, it can be a bit of a problem, right?

That's why, whether you're a recording songwriter or not, you should always have a hand-held cassette recorder loaded and ready to go. Believe it or not, Joe Pro Tools, there *is* a use for such low-tech gear. You only need something that can capture an idea instantly; it doesn't need to sound good (you can make it sound good later).

On a similar note, you might consider digging out your old 4-track or 8-track and using it instead of your digital rig for your Day Sessions. These devices were designed to be used as audio sketchpads, and with IMM, "sketching" is really all we need to do. The songwriting/recording process can go a lot faster when you use lower-tech machines, and anything that takes technological encumbrances out of your way is definitely a good thing.

Whatever the case, it's a crime to lose a song idea just because you can record at 96kHz and 24 bits—don't let it happen!

MOUTH MUSIC

START!

STUCK?

Using your mouth is often the fastest way to get a musical idea out of your head. (Your mouth is, you know, a hole that opens right out of your head, right?) Remember when you were 15 years old and you would tell your friends about this totally rockin' song you heard? You did a "scat singing" impression of the song using your mouth—something like, *Dur dur dur … Jnt Jnt Jurrrrrr! Dudududududud Bshh! Neeearrr! Fweee fwee Bshhh!* Or, think of the "horns" in the middle-eight section of the Beatles' "Lady Madonna": Rather than writing out lines for hired musicians to play, John, Paul, and George just *sang* the parts (a real sax solo was later added on top), and the "mouth horns" are now an inseparable part of that classic tune.

If you need to start a song or come up with a new part, just *come out and say* the musical idea you were trying to get at. *Sing something*—anything! Make percussion sounds, emit a blood-curdling scream, speak in tongues … it doesn't matter. The point is you created *something*, and that allowed you to move on. Once you've done that, you can transcribe the idea, or build a song around the actual recording you made, or do whatever you want with it. Remember, if you "hear" a melody when you're playing the 20-Song Game, you don't have to spend five minutes looking for an "appropriate" sound to express that melody. Just sing it!

FIELD RECORDING

START! Grab your handheld cassette recorder, go outside, and walk around recording stuff. Factory sounds. Squirrels. Playgrounds. Traffic—whatever. *Musique concrète.* Record the sound of a machine like a lawnmower, so that when you get back to your audio laboratory, you can turn it into a rhythm or a pitched keyboard sample. If you're feeling daring, walk up to people who are innocently sitting alone in an outside café, thrust the recorder in their face, and say, "Give me a song!" and record their baffled responses.

In accordance with the 20-Song-Game rules, it's okay to make field recordings anytime, as long as they aren't specifically musical—that is, as long as they're just raw ingredients for music that may be created sometime in the future. However, it's always nice when your field recordings happen on *the day of* your session. That way, they're truly part of the musical "diary entry" that is your Day Session—a document of the process you went through when you played the 20-Song Game. And it makes the Game more fun!

FIELD SINGING

START! On the day of your session, perhaps during your morning constitutional or as you're on your way to Jack in the Box to gear up for the session ahead, bring your handheld cassette recorder with you, and sing into it. Improvise songs or bits of songs, and sing them into your recorder. Don't be afraid to capture bits of mouth music (see above) as well. Then, take them home and use them to build songs, or transcribe them—whatever treatment you desire. It can also be a nice break in the *middle* of your session to go out for a walk and do a little field singing. (Your neighbors may think you've gone off your rocker, but don't let that stop you.) Variation: Before you sing something, put on a pair of headphones jacked into a metronome. This will give your recording a steady time base, making it easier to incorporate your actual improvisations into songs.

Field singing is a good general practice to adapt for catching stray song ideas when you are walking around, living your life. However, if you are using this technique in tandem with the 20-Song Game, and you want to play by the rules, remember to restrict your field singing to the *actual day* of the session.[1] The 20-Song Game is about writing music from scratch, and when you use the field-singing technique, you are producing actual *written* notes and rhythms, even lyrics. (See page 19, Rules of the 20-Song Game.)

USING TECHNOLOGY

Recording

One great thing about technology is that it isn't human, so it's immune to the foibles and predilections that can keep our human brains trapped in boxes of predictability and routine. In other words, you can use technology to bust out of ruts you may find yourself falling into. A technological transformation can be at once extremely easy to achieve and yet amazingly powerful at creating something new and inspiring. If you have the tools, why not use them to inject some freshness and variety into your Day Sessions?

RANDOM MIDI

For recording songwriters who can sequence MIDI: MIDI offers many ways to exploit randomness in starting new songs. You can plunk out

---

1. By all means, don't get so caught up in the Game rules that you prohibit yourself from using your handheld recorder outside of the 20-Song Game. Anytime you get an idea for a song, pick up the recorder and capture it! But if you do turn the idea into a song—whether it's during a Day Session or otherwise—be sure to tell your lodge that it's an "extra credit" song and not, strictly speaking, a product of the 20-Song Game.

a series of random notes on a keyboard, and then change the order, durations, pitches, or octaves of any (or all) of them until you come up with something that strikes you as musical. Or, you can draw random notes onscreen and work with them in similar ways. You can also get a non-pitched MIDI instrument (such as a drum machine) to trigger a sequence of random notes, and use that as a foundation to build on. And a few systems allow you to convert a piece of audio into MIDI. If the conversion isn't a straightforward one, the program may have to make its best guesses, with results that can be very random indeed—rich fodder for musical inspiration.

LOOP & SWITCH

START! Come up with a repeating pattern of notes on a MIDI keyboard; it doesn't have to be all that interesting. Then set up a repeating loop of these notes, or just play the pattern over and over. While the pattern is playing, start paging through the keyboard's sounds, or on a sampler or tone module that's slaved to the keyboard. Eventually you may hit upon a sound that fits perfectly with the loop—and the combination of the notes and the sound may immediately suggest a direction to go in next.

AUDIO DESTRUCTION

START! Pick a sound, any sound. (Something longer and more rhythmic, like a drum loop or a piano riff, works well.) Then use your technology to destroy, mangle, or otherwise make unrecognizable the sample. A few ideas: Boost it by 40dB to distort it into mere ashes. Flip it around into reverse. Cut it in half and swap the two halves, so it starts in the middle. Run it through a ring modulator plug-in or stomp box.

Then, loop your destroyed sound, put on a pair of headphones, and listen to it repeat. Keep your mind open and "listen" for ideas that could be added under, over, or before or after the loop. Consciously try to prevent notions of traditional rhythm or harmony from constraining what you do with your destroyed sound. So what if your idea for a second track is "wrong"? Whole movements in music began with a "wrong" idea. Let the sound you hear stimulate your open mind; don't let your mind close off the possibilities of where you can go with your new song.

UNUSUAL LOOPS

START! Similar to Audio Destruction (above), this one begins with an unusual sound or sound effect. Just loop it, listen to it for 15 or 30 seconds, and then start playing something over it. An interesting thing happens when your brain hears something repeat: It begins to interpolate within the sound, forming perceived patterns that perhaps aren't really there. Repetition makes your brain want to turn even a seemingly random sound into something that's easier to grasp. Since music is often built out of repeating patterns, a repeating sound very often becomes musical in some way—especially when you keep your mind open to new and unusual musical ideas.

FLIP SOMETHING AROUND

START! MIDI sequencing/recording programs make it easy to reverse the direction of a piece of audio or a passage of notes. You can start a song by **STUCK?** playing something quite boring and conventional and then reversing it—instant freshness. Or, record any piece of existing music, reverse it and perhaps loop it, and then play something on top of that. You can keep the reversed part in the mix—but to absolve yourself of potential copyright problems, delete it once you've added a few tracks. Or, start out by reversing something that's already yours—perhaps from the same Day Session. Either way, it's 100 percent original and all yours.

If you're stuck, try reversing one part of your arrangement, or perhaps the whole thing. Then play (or sing) something to accompany that, and finally, flip what you just played. If you recorded MIDI notes, the notes will then be in reverse; if you recorded audio, it will also *sound* backwards. This can be cool, but if you don't want that "backwards" sound, just transcribe what you're hearing, and then re-record it normally.

FOREGROUND TO BACKGROUND

STUCK? If you're working on a song and it doesn't seem to be going anywhere, and you need to move on—but you don't feel like just giving up on it— try pushing the music to the background and putting something new on top. For example, add a voice-over commenting on the music (see Self-Reflexive Songs, page 86), a new layer of audio that changes the meaning of what went before, sound design for a fake movie, etc. This way, the lame song you were working on simply becomes the "score" for something completely different. Forget about the music you were writing before; it's not important. Instead, focus on making the new layer of audio interesting, so that it carries the song.

INSTRUMENTATION & ARRANGEMENT

HAVE YOU EVER noticed the way setting eyes and ears on a nice-sounding instrument—say, a marvelously in-tune grand piano, or a crystalline 12-string guitar with new strings—can give you a powerful itch to sit down and write a song? While composition is definitely a thing that happens in your head, it can often happen that the simple prospect of playing an instrument that you like to play, or the prospect of finding out what *this* instrument and *that* instrument would sound like playing together, can be powerfully inspiring in itself, effectively luring you and your brain into the creative process. Sometimes the acoustic properties of an instrument, or the sound of two or more instruments playing together, will suggest a new musical direction, a mood, a key, a musical phrase, an orchestration effect—as if those instruments had minds of their own. The solutions in this section draw on the inspirational quality that certain instrumental tones and combinations exude, to influence the direction of your session and to motivate you as a songwriter.

THE FREEDOM OF ORCHESTRATION ACT

START! This is a great one for shaking stuff up: Purposefully set out to write a song that, for whatever reason, would be extremely impractical (or even impossible) for you to perform live. For example, write a cathedral-size arrangement involving boys' choir, an African percussion troupe, and a full string section. Or, write a piece of music that's well above your own instrumental skill level. (MIDI is a good way to do both of these things.)

This simple technique can be revolutionary for a songwriter who is used to writing music for a band. When you start worrying about how songs can be performed live, you can begin to dismiss good songwriting ideas out of hand, without even giving them a chance. It can get to the point where an entire dimension of your musical personality is relegated to the back burner for years, while you try to make this band thing happen. It doesn't have to be that way!

The thing is, whether or not a song is playable live is *not* more important than the musical potential of the song itself—and sometimes it's good to remind yourself of this very fact. So, write a song that completely ignores what is practical!

The wonderful thing about modern technology like samplers and laptops is that it's getting harder and harder to write a song that truly can't be played live. So don't let the merely *possible* get in the way of your impulses as an arranger. Have fun with it. Use your imagination. Go all the way! Later, you can figure out how to play the damn thing live.

NOVEL SOUNDS

START! Start from an instrumentation or recording approach that is interesting in itself, regardless of how it may end up sounding. For example, write something just to brag that you used "slide autoharp" in a song. Or, record a bass line by putting a contact mic onto a door, pressing the headstock of your bass against the door, and then playing something on the bass.[2] In other words, begin with a "novelty" instrumentation or songwriting approach set up so that no matter how the song turns out, it makes for a good story. Sometimes that's enough to make the song worth the effort.

PLAYING WITH TOYS

START! Great for parents: Write a song that's inspired by a sound from a toy that you already have. You can actually "play" the toy into a microphone, or you can sample each sound the toy makes, and either use the sounds directly in

---

2. The example of slide autoharp, and that whole contact mic/door/headstock trick, were both stolen from Michael Mellender, the king of gonzo arrangement anecdotes. ("So, I took a player piano, right? And then, I got this large-diaphragm mic, and—oh, yeah, the player piano was on fire, and there was this alligator lizard. So anyway . . . .")

songs, or electronically mess them up, or turn them into pitches, and use these samples to "spin off" ideas for a song. Whole Day Sessions can be done just by using toys that are lying around the house.

SWITCH THE SOUND

 If your existing arrangement of a song isn't doing anything for you, try simply changing one (or more) of the parts from one sound to another. This is easy if you're recording with MIDI: Just send the same MIDI notes to a different synth or sampler patch. Try a radical change—like, from Minimoog bass to bassoon, or even piccolo. How would that metal guitar riff sound if a horn section were playing it? Try it and find out! Even if the result isn't a brilliant artistic discovery, at least it will be *different*, and that alone may inspire you to take the song in an exciting new direction.

DOING STUFF YOU AREN'T SUPPOSED TO DO

A FUNNY THING can happen during an IMM session. In spite of the total freedom and mental privacy that the Game offers, and the fact that this isn't even "real" music, occasionally you start to make a musical decision, but an inner voice suddenly pops up and says, "Hey! You can't do that!"

Every time you play the 20-Song Game, you have an amazing opportunity to challenge your inner voice of authority, and to do stuff that you aren't supposed to do. The following techniques represent the most *drastic* solutions available within the IMM system for flying in the face of that little voice. If that voice were a schoolyard bully who gets in your way and says, "If you cross that line, something bad will happen," the three techniques in this section would be the rough equivalent of punching that bully in the neck, and crossing that line anyway.

THE CLEAN BREAK

 Sometimes, the only thing keeping you from ending a song, or getting from the beginning of the bridge to the last chorus, is the

formality that you are supposed to put a real ending, or a real bridge, in that spot. But when you're playing the 20-Song Game, there's no time—or need—for such formality.

So if you're stuck for a bridge or a chorus, or whatever, just make a *clean break*: Insert absolute silence, or a test tone, or noise, or any kind of random audio, into that part of the song. If you are having trouble with the ending, just let the audio abruptly *cut out*. This always gets a laugh at lodge meetings; your fellow lodgers will understand. You can write a bridge or an ending some other time.

THE "WORST CASE" OFFENSIVE

ONE OF THE most ironic things about the creative process is that sometimes, when you are trying your level best to avoid writing a bad song, it can start to get harder and harder to remember what a "good" song is supposed to sound like—until your mind has gone completely blank, preventing you from starting *any* kind of song.

Songwriting phobias can have this effect on a songwriter. You might be in the middle of a songwriting session, and suddenly you find yourself thinking, "Don't write something trite!" or, "Don't write something pretentious!" Pretty soon, you can't seem to think about anything else, until you've spent an hour and a half staring off into space, unable to write so much as a lick of music.

Here is a solution that has a kind of pleasing symmetry to it: Set a course directly into the center of what makes you nervous as a songwriter, and stage-dive right into the thick of it. Walk right up to the biggest, meanest, ugliest songwriting phobia you can find, tap it on its shoulder, and say, "You. Me. Outside."

STEAMROLLING

 For IMM users tangled up in a brutal case of mid-song block, where the entire songwriting process grinds to a halt, Steamrolling is a kind of ultimate weapon—a way to smash through that mental wall like a Mack truck through a cyclone fence.

Steamrolling means taking a song in a sudden, radical direction, and letting *nothing* get between you and finishing the song. Swerve off the *safe* path of songwriting, and take this song offroad, in the opposite direction of where it is "supposed" to go—something bold, daring,

In other words, purposely set out to write the *worst* song you possibly can.

Afraid of sounding trite? Write a song that takes triteness over the edge! Afraid of sounding pretentious? Write something that goes *beyond* pretentious! Take it to its logical extreme. Create a satire of that fear. Have *fun* with it. See for yourself, once and for all, where that road actually leads. Chances are, you'll discover that there was never anything there to be worried about.

This method can be an intensely liberating experience. Since it literally sets your expectations at a negative value, it can have the ironic effect of *freeing you*, drawing out the most bold, expressive, and personal music that your mind is capable of producing. In other words, you just might find out that writing a bad song on purpose is a lot harder than you originally thought.

The wonderful guarantee of this method is that no matter what happens, you win. If you actually succeed and write a bad song, you can always say, "I did that on purpose! Funny, huh?" and laugh about it with your friends. But, if you mess up and write a *really good* song, you can always say, "I meant to do that!"

ridiculous, wild, *illogical*. Write a funny ending to a serious song, write an *a cappella* chorus to your big guitar-rock song, or maybe even apply some effect or audio treatment that obliterates the existing tracks beyond recognition. Lay a field of electronic beeps over a country ballad, lay a laugh track over a beautiful piece of orchestral music—who knows what could happen? Anything! You might write the worst song you have ever written. You might write the best song you have ever written. But finish it!

Despite the volume-oriented rules of the 20-Song Game, sometimes a kind of reverence or preciousness can build up around a song while you are writing it. This can happen because a song seems to be going really well (and now you are worried about messing it up), or you might be working on a song that isn't so hot, and you get the feeling that you *could* make it into a great song, but you aren't sure how. Both of these feelings seem to dictate that you slow down, obsess on details, and ensure that this song turns out *just* right. This can create an increasing sense that there is a "right" way and a "wrong" way for that song to go—and before you know it, you've been working on the song for hours and hours and have painted yourself into a corner. A song like that can swallow up an entire session!

You'd think a problem that complicated would have a complicated solution, but this one— for a change—is simple. Those impulses commanding that you slow down, making sure that the song goes down the "right" path, are holding you back! Steamrolling is about flying in the face of those feelings, as *ruthlessly* and decisively as possible—taking the "wrong" path on purpose, so that you are free to move on.

When you are generating raw material, there is no "correct" or "incorrect" way to do it, right? Prove it! Forget everything you know, toss that rule book out the window, and *drive through* to the end of the song, by any means necessary. You can always fix a song later, and you can always write *more*. Who knows—you might be surprised just how *right* that song sounds when you listen to it the next day.

Session Themes

MAKE NO MISTAKE, playing the 20-Song Game is fun in itself—but it's also fun to spice up the Game with a *theme*. When you apply a theme to your Day Session, you are still playing the 20-Song Game—but you're playing it under certain conditions or restrictions, or with a particular goal in mind. By having a common element that ties the songs together, you may not need to invent each one out of absolute nothingness—which can make it easier to start songs, write lyrics, and so on.

WORKING ON YOUR OWN

THESE THEMES ARE for IMM songwriters working by themselves, although naturally, an entire lodge can use these themes, with each member working on them individually.

THE INFLUENCES SESSION

SOMETIMES WE'RE AFRAID to write songs that sound too much like our musical influences—it's one of those self-imposed (and socially reinforced) rules that hold us down as songwriters. But the IMM perspective on this is, do it anyway! On purpose! Do an entire session where you jump right in and make a *beeline* for your biggest influence or influences, and see where it takes you. Cross the line (see page 29) and write songs that sound *far too much* like your favorite group or musician.

SMASH STUFF TOGETHER

SIMILAR TO THE Influences Session (above), but in this theme, every song smashes together the sounds of two (or even three) musical acts. What would Dave Matthews sound like if he were in Duran Duran? What if Jimi Hendrix sat in with Green Day, with Chester Thompson drumming? Write some songs and find out!

THE MEMORY LANE SESSION

DEVOTE A SESSION to recreating music from the deepest recesses of your memory banks—music that you remember from your childhood. Pop songs, cartoon themes, music that your parents listened to … stuff that didn't necessarily influence you as a musician, but which helped to shape you as a *person*. You may find that plumbing these early, innocent impressions of music is a deeply enriching experience.

THE DAY MUSICAL

WRITE A SHORT musical in one day. You might start out by coming up with a list of characters and a broad plot outline, perhaps followed by ideas for song titles or lyrical themes to be explored. Keep in mind that it does not have to be a Broadway-type musical! In fact, the characters and plot devices can be totally nonsensical, and the songs don't necessarily have to hang together in a cohesive way. That's because when you're doing a revision (see Chapter 6), you might end up polishing up just a couple of these songs, completely rewriting their words, etc., making them totally unrelated to their original versions. The Day Musical theme just provides a device that you can use to spin songs off from, making the 20-Song Game more fun.

Also try: One-day operas, film scores, and concept albums.

THE I'VE-ALWAYS-WANTED-TO-DO-THAT SESSION

A DAY SESSION is the perfect opportunity to sketch out a musical project that you've wanted to do for a while but haven't found the time for. For example, maybe you want to do a song cycle about the molting habits of lobsters. (Who doesn't?) You may not want such a project to take up time that you could devote to "regular" songwriting—but you also might not want to abandon an idea like that without giving it a chance. A Day Session is a great way to test the waters and see if the concept is worth pursuing further.

METER-MADE SONGS

DO A SESSION where every song is in a different meter—for example, a song in three, a song in four, another in five, and so on. You can also double up the songs by using different time signatures—two songs in five, for instance, with one in 5/4 and another in 5/8.

THE 20-MELODY SESSION

BEGIN YOUR SESSION simply by writing 20 fairly developed melodies for one instrument (any instrument), and then write music (and perhaps words) to support each of those melodies. Check out the All About the Notes section (pages 70–75) for ideas on how to start and develop the melodies.

THE SPLIT START

THIS THEME CHALLENGES your ability to "forget" what you've done previously and keep your mind open to all musical possibilities. Start a song normally, and finish it normally. But then, go back to the beginning, identify what you think of as the "hook" of that song (the main riff, melody, or theme), and then envision an *alternate future* for that hook. Write a new song that uses the same starting point, but takes it in a completely new direction—as wildly different from the first version as possible.

For example, write a chord progression on guitar, develop it into a song, and then when you're done, go back and write two new songs based around that same guitar progression—but *these* songs incorporate two very different bass lines and drum beats, perhaps one of them in half-time or double-time. For an extra challenge, do a *third* version—or, if you're a true masochist, even more. Part of the fun of this theme is seeing if you can make each version unrecognizable from the others, except perhaps for the one element that they have in common.

THE GRAB & DIVERGE SESSION

WRITE YOUR FIRST song of the day, and then grab a single element from that song—it could be a few notes of a melodic line, two of the chords, etc.—and write your second song based on that element. For example, take one bar of the bass line from the song's B section, loop it, and write a song over that. Or, turn that bar of bass notes into the beginning of a new melody. Then, when you've written your second song, grab an element and write a third song based on that. Keep going until you reach 20. The cool thing about this is you always have something with which to start the next song—you don't have to create starts from scratch.

THE EXQUISITE CORPSE SESSION

WRITE AND/OR record your songs using the assembly-line approach (see page 26), but when you're coming up with a new part, write it in response to only one other part, not the whole arrangement. For example, record drum parts and bass lines for 20 songs, but then record guitar parts with the drums muted, and later, vocal melodies with the drums *and* bass muted (listening only to the guitar). The more layers you add on, the stranger—and often the more interesting—the result can be.

FILM RE-SCORING

CHOOSE A FILM that you know very well, and do a session where every song is a "score" for one scene in the movie, or is otherwise inspired by the scene. Be sure to turn down the sound so you aren't influenced by any score music that may exist in the scene. However, another approach is to turn up the sound and "re-imagine" the scene's score music, turning it into something original.

THE 20-MINUTE, 20-SECTION SONG

THE TITLE SAYS it all: You play the 20-Song Game, but each song is one minute long with its own key, tempo, and feel, and each song morphs smoothly into the song before it and after it—resulting in one giant "mega-song." Hint: Using the assembly-line songwriting approach (see page 26) is practically a must when tackling this task.

WORKING WITH OTHERS

THESE THEMES ARE for two or more people working in collaboration. In most cases it's preferable if both are doing their sessions on the same day, but most of these themes can be adapted in cases where that isn't possible.

THE TRACK SWAP

THIS IS A blast. Before you do a session, coordinate with another lodge member. Agree that you'll each start a bunch of songs and then hand them over to the other person, who will proceed to finish them. This way, each person spends roughly half of a session starting songs and the other half finishing them. "Starting" can be as simple as writing a title, concept, words only, or hook, or it can mean almost completing a song and sending the recorded tracks to the other person via e-mail. In either case, each participant should contribute something significant to each song. Don't play the results for each other until the actual lodge meeting. Hearing what someone else did to your start can be a real ear-opener, and even a mind-blower! Exquisite Corpse variation: Give the other song-writer only *one part* of the arrangement, and ask them to add onto the song based only on what they're given.

ONE START, TWO FINISHES

THIS IS SIMILAR to the Track Swap, but the results can be even more mind-boggling (and inspiring). In this theme, three lodge members coordinate their sessions. Each member starts a few songs, and then the other two members finish them—*independently*. The result is two different versions of every song, with some element or elements in common. To enhance the experience, you might agree that one person will finish the song in a more conventional or predictable way, and the other will go in a very different direction. At the meeting, of course, play the two versions consecutively. It's fascinating to hear two independent interpretations of one start.

ONE START, EVERYONE FINISHES

IDENTICAL TO ONE Start, Two Finishes—except the entire lodge gets involved with every song. Each member starts one to three songs, and everyone else finishes them independently. Because there are so many finishes for each start, this theme works best if the starts are minimal—perhaps just a brief vocal hook or a single loop—thereby allowing the finishes to go in radically divergent directions.

TRIBUTE TO LODGEMATES

IF YOUR LODGE HAS been around for a while, you probably have an intimate understanding of each member's songwriting style. As a session theme, have everyone in the lodge do a session in the style of someone else in the lodge—or, each of you can do one song in the style of each member. It's always fun hearing someone do an "impersonation" of your music, and it can also shed light on your style and its strengths and weaknesses.

THE TELEPHONE DOUBLE-BLIND

ON THE DAY of a session, you and a lodgemate coordinate by phone and attempt to write one of the songs from your session together, using only *verbal* phone communication to coordinate the writing. You split the writing chores for that song *in half*, and each endeavors to write his half without hearing what the other guy is doing. Near the end of the session, the two of you meet and assemble the two halves into one song.

It goes like this: Each of you can tell the other guy general stuff about your side of the song—for example, you can say, "It's a vamp on *Gm6*, it has an ambient feel, and it's at 120 beats per minute"—but you can't play your music over the phone to him. So while you know that the other guy is writing something in the right key, and it's at the right tempo, and maybe even that it's in a comparable style or mood, you basically have no idea what his half really sounds like. You leave the rest up to chance!

The song can be split in half with you writing, say, the first minute-and-a-half of the song, and the other guy writing the second half. It can also be cut in half with you writing, say, drums and bass, and the other guy writing another layer of the song (say, guitar and vocals), which will eventually be laid down *on top* of what you wrote. You could also divide up the song into little sections; maybe you write the verses and the other person writes the choruses.

If there is a lodge meeting at the end of the night, remember to schedule your sessions to allow for a time cushion, so that after you get together and assemble your song, you'll still have enough time to make it to the *big* meeting.

It is scary how much fun this can be.

While the example above provides instructions for coordinating *one* of your songs, keep in mind that you and a lodgemate can coordinate multiple songs out of a session—as many as you want! (Twenty songs sounds really hard, though.)

THE ARTIST-FRIEND SESSION

GO MULTIMEDIA! Coordinate a session with a friend who's a fine artist (illustrator, painter, etc.). Ask the person to create ten pieces of art, while you create ten pieces of music. Midway through the session, swap your stuff—give your friend your ten songs in exchange for the ten drawings. For the rest of your session, write ten songs inspired by the drawings, while your friend makes ten drawings inspired by your songs.

Special Games

THESE ARE IMM-TYPE games that fall outside the rules and other specifics of the 20-Song Game. The goals are similar, though: to create a lot of musical ideas in a specific amount of time. You can play a special game with one other lodgemate in a Day Pact (see page 50), or with your entire lodge in a "special session" that allows people to break from the 20-Song Game's restrictions in what is essentially a lodge-wide Day Pact. You can also play special games simply by yourself.

While special games are fun and valuable, remember to devote most of your lodge meetings to sharing the results of the 20-Song Game. The 20-Song Game is sort of the active ingredient of the IMM system—the unifying factor that ties it all together—and it's the most effective game in this book for smashing through mental obstacles, and growing as a songwriter in the process. Always returning to the 20-Song Game also helps to keep the playing field level and to prevent meetings from devolving via the "open-mic effect" (see page 52).

THE BACK-BURNER GAME

SPEND A WEEK writing music entirely in your head—don't write down or record anything. Then, at the end of the week, spend a day turning your ideas from that week into recorded or written-down songs. The beauty of this game is that it forces you to compose songs based only on music and lyrics that you can remember over a period of time. Since your brain weeds out the less interesting material, the resulting music is automatically more memorable.

THE TWO-DAY GAME

THIS ESSENTIALLY COMBINES a one-day text-only writing binge with a session of the 20-Song Game, in a two-day session. On the first day, spend an entire 12-hour period writing lyrics, poems, short stories, haikus, or whatever else you can think of. This is really fun to do with another person, split up and coordinating via e-mail, while drinking an entire pot of coffee. Every time you write something, you can e-mail it off to your friend, and get a reply right back—and vice versa. Instant gratification! Then, on the second day, write music that draws exclusively from the lyrics or writings you did the day before. As a variation, coordinate a lyric-swap with another player: On the first day, each of you writes lyrics only, and on the second day, you swap material and you each write music using only the other guy's lyrics.

THE SEVEN-DAY (WOODSHEDDING) GAME

HERE'S A WAY to stretch your abilities as an instrumentalist as well as a songwriter. On the first day, write a piece of music (or several) that pushes your technical abilities on an instrument to the absolute limit. Deliberately write things that you would otherwise avoid, simply because you can't actually play them. (For recording songwriters, MIDI sequencing is a great way to do this.) Then, for the next five days, woodshed (practice) like crazy on that piece of music until you can play it as best as you possibly can. On the seventh day, either record yourself playing the piece with your newfound chops, or perform it live for your lodgemates or for friends and family.

THE OPUS GAME

CHALLENGING: DO A session consisting of just a single piece of music, but make it a complex one with lots of different sections, or layers. For example, your opus could be a 15-minute aria about the fall of Rome, or a musical sitcom episode. This is different from the Day Musical session theme (see page 100) in that you're specifically trying to make a bunch of parts fit together into one big "song."

THE MERGING GAME

THIS IS SIMILAR to the session theme called One Start, Two Finishes (see page 103), except in this game, rather than creating two different songs from each start, you and your lodgemate join forces at the end of your session and attempt to create *one song* from each start, incorporating only elements that the two of you had written separately. For example, you may decide that songwriter A had a better guitar part and drum beat, and that songwriter B had a better bass line and vocals. Depending on whether you went in similar or different directions with a start, crafting a song from these parts can be either a snap or an intense challenge. Either way, it's a unique method for combining your talents to create new and interesting sounds. Tip: For certain types of starts, recording songwriters may want to specify the tempo and/or key of the song being created; otherwise it might be too difficult to make one guy's parts fit with the other guy's.

THE SUBTRACTION GAME

THIS IS THE musical equivalent of sculpting in stone rather than clay or wax. For the first half of a session, write a whole bunch of musical parts, one on top of the other and in the same tempo and key—like four drum beats, five bass lines, three guitar riffs, and so on. Write *far* too many parts; create an absolute orchestration disaster. Making a huge mess is part of the fun! For this to be useful, though, all of these parts should conform to a central groove, or some other aspect that lets them coexist—that is, unless you want to make things difficult for yourself, or you want your music to be more "out." When you're finished, start *subtracting out* parts to see what you can sculpt out of this solid mass of music. Chisel it down to one song or song idea, and then start over and see what happens when you chisel out an entirely different song. Insert rests wherever you want, and feel free to move parts around or transpose them—but once you finish creating the initial "solid mass," don't add anything new. In addition to being a game for creating song ideas, this is a great way to learn about using space and economy in a piece of music.

SPOOLING

IF YOU ARE a pop or rock songwriter/arranger interested in branching out into the more compositional side of things—creating music with themes that grow, multiply, layer, and evolve over time—this game is a great introduction. Spooling is a musical-association game. It can produce extremely complex and diverse results, sort of the way you might make a list of free-associated words (see Chain & Compare, page 78) and then see where that takes you. However, the method itself is a simple proposition.

Spooling is similar to the Grab & Diverge session theme (see page 101), where you write a song, and when you are done, you grab a little piece of the song and create a new song based on that piece. But in spooling, the "changeroo" doesn't happen when one song ends and another starts up—it happens in between song *sections*, the goal being to create a single piece of music that continually blends or morphs from one section to the next, each section liquidly re-appropriating a theme from the last one.

Let's say you create a block of music, something that sounds like the main groove of a song; it's a repeating pattern of drums, a bass line, a guitar line, and some keyboard strings. Normally, after you were done writing that main groove, you might think, "Okay, time to write a chorus." In spooling, you don't do that! Instead, you grab something out of the main groove part you just wrote—maybe you grab the string melody, or the arpeggiated pattern you played on guitar—and you create a new section of music using that little scrap as the starting point. The new section may have a completely different feel, tempo, or meter. You can alter, invert, stretch, or dice up that chunk from the previous section—although it's a cool effect when the listener can actually hear the old "theme" being re-appropriated. It can also be fun (and useful) to create five successive sections that audibly demonstrate different ways you can use just one bass line or melody.

This game creates a "spool" of free-associated music sections; instead of trying to settle into a "normal" song, each successive section continues to expand, alter, morph, and seek different ways to look at an introductory theme.

An interesting thing can happen when you are spooling: The sections you create keep getting further and further "out," but then, suddenly, you come *full circle*. You arrive at a new section that reminds you of some earlier section—and if you compare them, you may realize that the new section would sound great superimposed over that old section. All of a sudden, you've generated this really solid song idea or "hook." You now have the option to grab those two sections out of the spool and use them in one of your "real" songs.

COMPOSER TENNIS

THIS IS THE multi-player version of spooling. It can be amazingly fun to take turns writing sections of music with another songwriter, where each time one of you gets a turn, he tries his level best to pull the rug out from under the other guy's section of music. One of you might say, "I'll liquefy your bass line into a piccolo part in 5/8!" And the other guy says, "Oh yeah? I'll turn your guitar line into an inverted harpsichord part, and I'll make the entire thing four times slower!"

Composer Tennis a great way for two songwriters to examine different sides of a musical idea, and it can be a highly valuable form of creative collaboration, where the two of you create music out of a continuous mental fabric that you have spun together. It can also be fun to treat it like a competitive sport, where you are both struggling to outdo each other, bringing out the best in each other in the process. It can end up turning into a hook-writing competition, where you're each trying to come up with some of the catchiest material you've ever written. Then, when you're done, both of you are free to grab the best of those ideas and use them in new songs. The potential is pretty much limitless.

THE COVERS GAME

FOR A CHANGE of pace, recording lodges can designate a "covers only" session, in which members make Immersion Music-style cover versions of other people's songs (either those of other lodge members or other artists' songs). To encourage creativity, the emphasis should be on radical change; think Devo's version of "Satisfaction." Some ideas for making a really out-there cover: Try keeping the words and melody but changing the chord progression, or keep the words and chords but change the melody. Or, try to fit the verse words and melody into the chorus and vice versa. Or, try to fit together the words and melody of one song into the chords of another song by the same artist, or a similar variation. Explore the possibilities!

ALBUM SHADOWING

PICK ONE OF your favorite albums of all time, and do a session where each song of yours "shadows" its numerical equivalent on the album in some way. For example, if the first song on the album is a catchy hit with a reggae feel, try to write a song that's a catchy "hit" with a reggae feel (but is otherwise completely different from the album cut). Continue this way and "shadow" every song, in order, resulting in an "album" of your own with a contour that broadly resembles the one that you shadowed.

THE POLISH GAME

SOMETIMES, IMMERSION MUSIC writing doesn't leave much energy for refining and finishing your best songs. A solution: Make the refining and finishing part of the game. For one session, everyone in the lodge (or just yourself) chooses some of their favorite songs from past Day Sessions to polish up—perhaps not to a "finished" level, just better. We can get bogged down by conventional songwriter baggage even when we're polishing songs, so having to tune up five or ten previously sketched-out songs can make the process more of a game. (See Chapter 6 for more on revising and polishing.)

THE 30-DAY (REVISION) GAME

THIS IS EXACTLY what it sounds like. Two or more players have 30 days to edit, refine, transplant, reinvent, replace, chop, paste, and otherwise tweak and obsess their fevered little guts out on music they've made in IMM sessions. At the end of the 30 days, there's a revision meeting. Everyone brings a nice, polished album of revised music, and they swap stories about this or that leg cramp that someone got on the seventh straight day that they edited the same three seconds of music.

The nice thing about the 30-Day Game is that while it provides an optimal situation for revising and presenting a bunch of old material, it can also be used for things other than revision. *Anything* is welcome at a 30-Day Game meeting, as long as you made it during the previous 30 days. You can use that whole month to play or invent any number of special games—games that take longer than one day to play. You can use the whole month to create some unimaginably complicated opus, finish a couple of songs that you've been working on for years, create a dense multimedia presentation, or create something that sounds like a totally polished album. The possibilities are wide open!

THE EXTENSION GAME

THIS IS ANOTHER revising and polishing game—it helps you develop previous song ideas, generate variations, and create new sections. Choose one, two, or three of your Day Session songs, and spend an entire day coming up with at least five variations on each—perhaps two different bridges, a couple of new riffs in the same tempo, key, and feel, and maybe a rideout or two (with a twist on the original chord progression). Proceed in *exactly* the same fashion that you would if you were playing the 20-Song Game—don't think, and don't edit yourself as you go. Just keep moving forward, and let those ideas spew. Later, you can decide which new ideas work with your original ideas.

THE CHILLA GAME

FOR IMM EXTREMISTS! *Chilla* is a North Indian rite of passage in which a musician plays his instrument for 40 days straight in total isolation. Similarly, as a once-in-a-lifetime, life-changing experience, play the 20-Song Game every day for *40 days*, with the aim to create a grand total of *800* original songs. Is it possible? We don't know—nobody in the ICS has ever tried it. But it's fun to think about!

INVENT YOUR OWN GAMES!

AFTER YOU'VE BEEN an IMM songwriter for a while, and you've done a few session themes and played some special games, you may find that you're developing a deep, almost scientific understanding of how your musical ideas form and develop. At that point, you will likely find yourself inventing your own session themes and special games to play. That's great! In fact, you can consider the games we've described here as mere *examples* of the things you can do with IMM. Get creative! When you do come up with a special game, discuss it informally with your lodgemates before a meeting—if they get excited about your idea, they may all want to try playing it.

Revising & Polishing Songs

WE HOPE THE first five chapters of *The Frustrated Songwriter's Handbook* have given you the tools to generate lots and lots of new songs and song ideas. But you probably didn't become a songwriter just to come up with minute-and-a-half song sketches and 30-second choruses with no verses. You probably want to write complete, fully developed songs with rich, juicy lyrics.

Fortunately, the really hard part is over. When you're writing a song, once you've come up with a broad sketch, a rough lyric, or a super-catchy chorus, you're almost all of the way to the top of the mountain. And when you have a stash of several dozen (or maybe a lot more) "body parts" for songs, all of which *you wrote* and *own forever*, the practice of creating "real" songs is just a matter of sifting through them, piecing elements together, and making some prudent changes and additions here and there.

The actual nitty-gritty of crafting finished songs—harmonic and melodic theory, meter, shades of lyrical meaning—is an enormous subject and well beyond the scope of this book. Plenty of other resources are available to help you, and we encourage you to seek them out. But we will say this: There are millions of ways to write songs, and as a songwriter you are an *artist*— so unless you're writing for a specific context where there are established conventions for songs (such as blues or country), the road for you is wide open. Everything is possible. Even if a book tells you that you shouldn't move from an *E* major chord to a *C* minor tonic chord, don't let that put the kibosh on an idea you have—one that just possibly could lead to the Next Big Thing in music. They're *your* songs—take them wherever you want to take them!

SORTING THROUGH YOUR RAW MATERIAL

LET'S SAY YOU'VE played the 20-Song Game a few times and have 50 solid song ideas. Obviously, the next thing you need to do is decide which of those ideas are worth developing. A great place to start this process is to think back to the lodge meetings where you played this material. Which of the songs got the biggest reactions? In addition to that, there are always songs that your lodgemates may not have gone crazy over, but which you just *love*. If you have IMM songs like this, by all means consider developing those ideas as well.

Another good approach is to put your IMM songs on a "limited edition" CD, give the CD to friends and family, and then ask them which of the songs jumped out as being especially enjoyable, or worthy of further development. You can remix or polish them a bit first, and you can restrict the song selection to only the better half or two-thirds of your IMM collection—but you also may choose not to limit yourself in this way. Sure, some of your IMM songs may seem unfit to show to the outside world, and let's face it, certain songs are obvious throw-it-in-the-dumpster flops. But it's also possible that out of 50 IMM songs, the best two or three are songs that you consider throwaways, or even too embarrassing to play for anyone outside the lodge. Is there any chance that you might trash one of these songs before the world tells you it could blossom into something really special? That possibility is always there. So, you might want to put all but the biggest clunkers on that "limited edition" CD. That way they all get a shot at being discovered by the world.

DEVELOPING SONG IDEAS

THE 20-SONG GAME tends to produce a lot of songs between one and two minutes in length, each consisting of maybe one verse and one chorus. For most popular-music formats, of course, songs around four minutes are more standard. If you're shooting for songs around that length, you'll obviously need to do some more work—you probably don't want to just repeat the first verse three times. (Although R.E.M. did that at least once, and as the Violent Femmes pointed out, sometimes the third verse *can* be the same as the first!)

If you have a good verse and chorus, then developing your song can be a matter of simply writing new words for additional verses and then repeating the chorus a few times. But if you have only a verse and no chorus, or vice versa, developing a song is a bit more involved—and, of course, songs commonly have other sections, such as a bridge, pre-chorus, guitar-solo section (perhaps similar to the verses but with an altered chord progression), intro, and/or outro.

One way to write additional sections is to grind them out in a conventional songwriting session, where you sit there with a pad of manuscript paper and a guitar, or in front of the piano, and try different things to see what works and what doesn't. But to make the process less laborious and more fun, how about making this part of the songwriting process a *game*, too? The Extension Game (see page 111) is a way to build on previous ideas and work up new sections of songs. Every once in a while, consider pulling out some of your Day Session songs and playing this game as part of either a Day Pact (see Chapter 4) or as a special game for your entire lodge. Similarly, you can write additional lyrics, or revise or replace existing placeholder lyrics, by scheduling for yourself a Day Session where you write lyrics only.

PUTTING IT ALL TOGETHER

NOW THAT YOU have, say, a great verse and chorus (from your original Day Session) plus lyrics for additional verses, a couple of potential bridges, a variation or two on the chorus, and several other pieces that take the song in different directions, here comes the *really* fun part: mixing and matching, seeing which parts work together and which don't, and coming up with a final song structure. A digital audio workstation (e.g., a recording program on a computer) is ideal for this, but for paper-and-pencil songwriters, the process is similar. Just start sticking sections together, like Lego blocks, and listen to how each section leads (or doesn't lead) into the next. If you came up with three bridges during an Extension Game, you'll appreciate being able to choose among them. Don't rule out more ambitious arrangements, such as giving the song two bridges or two types of choruses—it just might be the thing that turns your good song into a great one!

If you are recording on a DAW, finishing the song is a simple matter: just assemble the already-recorded parts into the structure you've decided on, smooth over the transitions (you may need to write new transitional segments to improve the flow from one section to another), and re-record performances where appropriate (see below). If you work on a linear format such as analog tape, you may need to re-record everything, but it's also possible to transfer your tracks to a friend's DAW and assemble the song there.

COMBINING IMM SONGS

WHEN YOU PLAY the 20-Song Game, often you come up with two or more songs that have something in common: a similar feel, chord progression, or maybe just the key or tempo. When you're revising, look for similarities between songs, and see if perhaps you could stitch together entire songs (or pieces of songs) to create a more developed piece of music—for instance, borrowing from one song for the verses and another song for the choruses.

Then there's the school of thought that says, why do the pieces have to be *similar*? Throughout the years, a lot of great songs have been built out of sharply contrasting elements. Think of "Layla," with its earlier rockin' portion followed by the piano-driven segment, or "Band on the Run," which has two very different "false starts" before the "real" song begins. "A Day in the Life" famously was written in two parts, the beginning/ending by John and the middle by Paul. In all of these cases, the songs' writers made rock & roll history by cobbling together very different song elements, creating something that was much stronger than any of their individual elements. So, when developing your songs, keep an open mind and try *anything* and *everything*. Every song presents so many opportunities and possibilities—don't let one of them pass you by simply because you didn't give it a chance.

MAKE AN ALBUM PACT

IF YOU'D LIKE to use the benefits of IMM (like peer pressure and support) to help you create an album or other large work, consider forming an Album Pact with someone. This is a long-term agreement between two or more lodge members—or just songwriting friends—that each of them will revise and polish an album's worth of songs over the course of a specific time period. It's almost like they're breaking off and forming their own "sub-lodge," but this kind of lodge is devoted to producing music for actual release. The participants can schedule Day Sessions, have regular meetings, and so on, just like a regular lodge. The end result, of course, is an album of wonderfully polished music by each participant, finished at around the same time.

GO AHEAD, GET PERFECT

IN POPULAR MUSIC there's been an on-and-off movement against perfectionism—you know, the whole 1970s punk-rock aesthetic that favors "raw" sounds over sterile, refined ones. When you play the 20-Song Game—regardless of whether you are writing garage rock or symphonic prog-rock—it might even be said that your brain undergoes a process of creative revolt that is not unlike the London Punk revolution: jettisoning perfectionism in favor of approaches that are more immediate.

However, at least in certain musical styles, there's a lot to be said for *crafting* music—honing and shaping every last element until a song is exactly the way you want it. And in many ways it makes sense; after all, how can a person create a great piece of finished art unless their self-expectations are extremely high? If you're this kind of songwriter—the kind who won't rest until you're certain a song is so good that it will make the listener lose all muscular control and collapse like a sack of rivets—then the revision and polishing stage is your chance to run riot!

This book is not part of any "anti-perfectionism" movement. The 20-Song Game is just a tool, not a philosophy, not a way of life. The Immersion Composition Society was not created to lower the expectations of its members to something more "realistic." Yech! The founding members of the ICS were, and continue to be, hopeless idealists with utterly unrealistic expectations—and this book was written as a way to look after our own. We *love* busy arrangements, songs that cram in a hundred changes, and obsessively tinkered production. We are all about that stuff! That is why, when we're talking about your "real" music, we'll never ask you to change your attitude or lower your expectations. Keep reaching! Keep attempting the impossible! When you get stuck, this book will be here to help you get unstuck, so that you can go back to being an unrealistic idealist again.

For natural perfectionists, fighting perfectionism can be a hell of a battle. But now that you've let go and generated a ton of raw material, it's time to let go in a different way and be as freakishly, tweakishly perfectionistic as you want. Spend a week on a line of a lyric to get the shades of meaning exactly right. Zoom your recording program in to the sample level and make that edit seamless. Pitch-correct, if you wish. Change melodies. Line up tracks. Add sections. Remix and remix. Indulge yourself! Because when you combine the power of IMM-generated raw material with your natural attention to artistic detail, you have the potential to do truly great things as a songwriter.

IT MAY NOT NEED POLISHING

IMM MAY BE a new way for you to write music—but actually, over the years there have been a lot of really famous songs that were written and even recorded in an IMM-like fashion. Ray Charles wrote his classic "What'd I Say" in front of a live audience, while playing a dance-a-thon, after he and his band had run out of material. Many Rolling Stones songs, like "Shattered," were written in studio jams while Keith and Ron riffed, Mick improvised, and the tape rolled. The Beatles recorded almost all of the "White Album" in long sessions lasting well into the early morning hours, while Abbey Road's brand-new 8-track machine captured their free-wheeling sonic experiments. (Okay, we promise, that's our last Beatles reference!) And Steely Dan … well, maybe not. The point is, in rock & roll history there are countless examples of vocal or instrumental performances that were invented on the fly—IMM-style—and which made it all the way to the song's final version, eventually becoming an integral part of our cultural tapestry.

In all of these cases, savvy musicians and producers recognized a *spark* of some kind in the music—something that was as good as, or better than, anything that could result from a formal, labored songwriting or recording session. It's a spark of spontaneity, of the artist being in the moment and expressing a genuine performance. That's precisely what makes many of these songs great.

Hey, guess what? That spontaneous *spark* is exactly what IMM creates, almost automatically and by design, in your own music. A lot of times, the stuff you come up with during a Day Session has a near-audible sense of play and abandon, as well as an authenticity, that you might not be able to capture in your more "careful" songwriting moments. So, in your quest to polish up your songs and make them more presentable to the public, try to keep an open mind. People in the outside world may actually prefer the "rough" version of your song to the "polished" version.

Sometimes, just letting a song sit for a week, or a month, makes it possible to listen to it with fresh ears. That out-of-time vocal phrase that bothered you so much in your IMM version may sound *just right* when you listen to it a month later. For recording songwriters, unless a performance has unwanted distortion or is otherwise unusable, consider not trying to recreate it in your polished version, even if the singing or playing isn't technically great. A remix may be all it takes to make that "flawed" performance shine. If you do decide to redo something, compare the "demo" and "polished" versions, and ask others for their opinions. Sometimes, the "demo" version will simply be better. That's just the way it is.

THE LIFE CYCLE OF THE IMMERSION SONGWRITER

FOR THOSE OF us in the Immersion Composition Society who have been practicing IMM for a long time, we've noticed a kind of "life cycle" that tends to accompany the method. You do volume songwriting for quite a few months (perhaps over a year if IMM is new to you), in the process generating a lot of exciting raw material for songs. At the same time, the immersive qualities of the Day Sessions allow you to acquire skills of various kinds. You have revelations and breakthrough moments, and you learn to make musical decisions fast—*really* fast. Almost automatically, you develop a deep-rooted desire to expand your IMM-born skills to areas that may be very dear to you, such as making perfectly arranged orchestrations, carefully crafted singer/songwriter ballads, or highly polished recordings. Given the insight into quality and detail that you gained by playing the 20-Song Game, you start to wonder, "What if I used an IMM-inspired approach not only to generate raw material, but also to craft my finished, 'real' music?" Meanwhile, there's a huge pile of keeper song ideas calling out, "Finish us! Finish us!" from the corner of the room.

So, at some point you often enter a phase where volume songwriting gives way to more fine-tuned musical pursuits. But that "itch" to play the 20-Song Game remains—so when you finish that album, or that opera, it's back to volume songwriting again.

And so goes the life of the Immersion songwriter.

Find out more about the Immersion Composition Society at our website: www.ics-hub.org. There, you can read about ICS lodges and personnel, hear examples of music and media from ICS members, and post your own session themes, special games, or links to your own lodge sites.

So, play, and be free!

ABOUT THE AUTHORS

KARL CORYAT (a.k.a. "Eddie Current") is the author of *Guerrilla Home Recording* [Backbeat Books] and is a consulting editor for *Bass Player* magazine, where he was a staff editor for 14 years. He has been producing recordings and creating original music since the 1980s, most recently as a founding member of the Immersion Composition Society's Wig Lodge (www.wiglodge.com).

NICHOLAS DOBSON started writing music when he was 11. In spring 2001, he came up with the idea for the Immersion Composition Society (www.ics-hub.org), along with co-founder Michael Mellender. Nicholas resides in West Oakland, California, in a dingy warehouse next to an aluminum recycling plant.

INDEX

Sugar Hill Gang, 84
support, 44–46
Switch the Sound method, 95

T

technology, using, 90–93
Telephone Double-Blind theme, 104–105
template files, 32–34
tension, 81
themes. *See* session themes
Three-Minute Burn, 24–25, 30
titles, song, 72
toys, playing with, 94–95
track numbers, 25
Track Swap theme, 103
tracks
    audio instruments, 32
    muting of, 75
    soloing, 75
    swapping, 103
    template files, 32
    vocal, 32
transposition, 74
Tribute to Lodgemates theme, 104
Two-Day Game, 106–107

V

verses, 115
Violent Femmes, 115
vocal tracks, 32
Vonnegut, Mark, 41

W

websites
    Ex'pression College for Digital Arts, 8
    ICS lodges, 61, 120, 121
    Immersion Composition Society, 120
"What'd I Say," 118
"White Album," 118
"Wig Lodge," x, 45, 61, 121
woodshedding, 107
"Wooly Bully," 80
writer's block. *See* creative block

Z

zero gravity, 20–21